Handbook of
Mediterranean Roman Pottery

Handbook of Mediterranean Roman Pottery

John W. Hayes

Published for the Trustees of the British Museum by

BRITISH MUSEUM PRESS

NOTE ON SPELLING OF NAMES

Where ancient names are cited in the text and appear on the map, the Latin form is used for Italian sites, but the Greek spelling (transliterated) for most sites in the East of the Empire, where Greek remained the common language for written texts. (Greek *k* counted as the equal of the Latin *c*, and the Greek ending *-os, -on* as the Latin *-us, -um*.) Anglicised versions appear where these are familiar: e.g. Corinth, Rhodes.

© 1997 The Trustees of the British Museum
First published in 1997 by British Museum Press
A division of The British Museum Company Ltd
46 Bloomsbury Street, London WC1B 3QQ

ISBN 0–7141–2216–5
A catalogue record for this book is available
from the British Library

Line illustrations by John W. Hayes
Photography by the British Museum Photographic Service
Map by Technical Art Services
Designed by Behram Kapadia in Palatino and Gill
Printed in Great Britain by The Bath Press

Contents

We wish to record the most noble and miraculous artefact that was made of it. From this vases were made for many occasions by the most noble and skilled Craftsmen of old of that noble city of Arezzo where we were born. . . . When, in our time, one for some reason dug within the city or round about, up to two miles away, great quantities of these pieces of vases were found. . . buried for well over a thousand years, and found so colourful and fresh, as if just made, so as to confound the experts with pleasure. . . When one of these pieces came into the hands of sculptors or draughtsmen or other experts, they would hold them as if they were sacred objects, amazed that human nature could rise to such delicacy. . . and would say that those Craftsmen were divine or that those vases came down from heaven.

Ser RISTORO OF AREZZO, MS of 1282
(For the original version, see G. Pucci in A. Vannini,
Museo Nazionale Romano, Le ceramiche V.2, 1988)

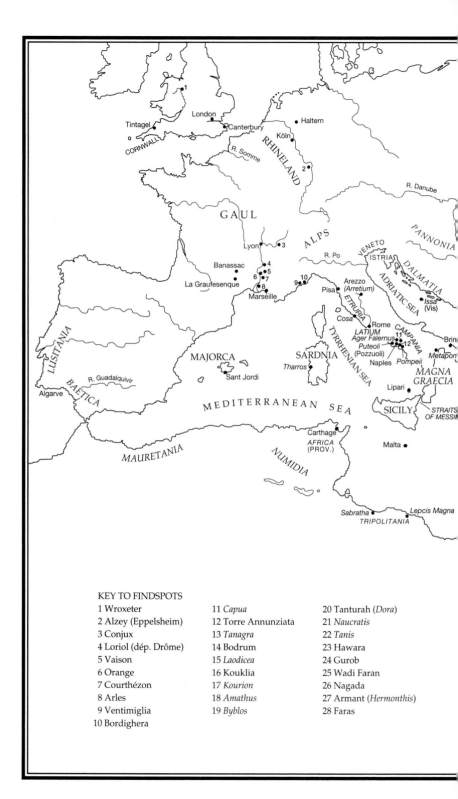

KEY TO FINDSPOTS

1 Wroxeter	11 *Capua*	20 Tanturah (*Dora*)
2 Alzey (Eppelsheim)	12 Torre Annunziata	21 *Naucratis*
3 Conjux	13 *Tanagra*	22 *Tanis*
4 Loriol (dép. Drôme)	14 Bodrum	23 Hawara
5 Vaison	15 *Laodicea*	24 Gurob
6 Orange	16 Kouklia	25 Wadi Faran
7 Courthézon	17 *Kourion*	26 Nagada
8 Arles	18 *Amathus*	27 Armant (*Hermonthis*)
9 Ventimiglia	19 *Byblos*	28 Faras
10 Bordighera		

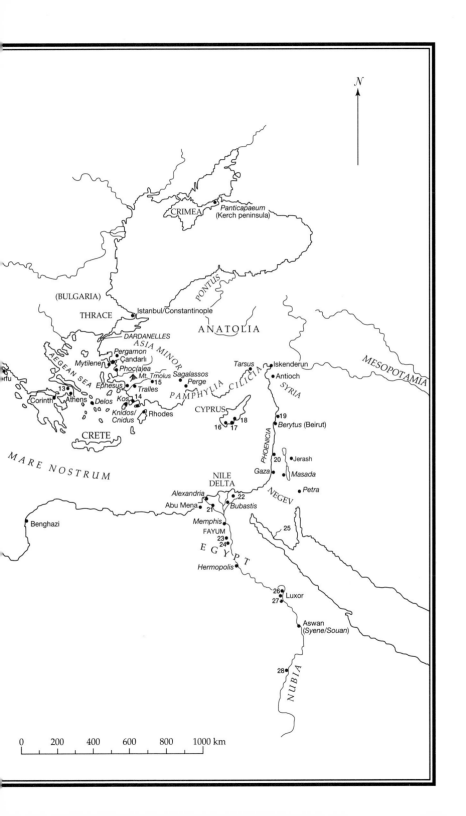

Acknowledgements

The initial suggestion to me to write this Handbook came from Dr Susan Walker, Deputy Keeper of the Department of Greek and Roman Antiquities in the British Museum, who has supported the project during the various stages of preparation (col. pl. II and pl. 14 reproduce illustrations from her handbook *Roman Art*). It was she who encouraged me to contribute the necessary line drawings – a number already have a thirty-year history, and have appeared in print elsewhere. Her colleagues Dr Donald Bailey and, more recently, Dr Paul Roberts (who has provided drawings for figs 8.2 and 25.9) have offered advice and practical assistance on numerous occasions. The staff members of the five British Museum departments holding material illustrated here (see p. 95, n. 1) are thanked for arranging study facilities (including long sessions in the Museum's basements and reserves), searching inventories, ordering photographs and the like. All the final photographs reproduced have been supplied by the BM Photographic Service. The cheerful collaboration and encouragement of Nina Shandloff (a Senior Editor at British Museum Press), who has had the unenviable task of chasing an author more often absent from Britain than at home, is much appreciated; I thank all at the Press, including the designer Behram Kapadia and copy editors Anne Marriott and John Banks, for co-ordinating the final stages of a rather complex publication within pressing time limits.

J. W. Hayes
Oxford
16 *February* 1997

INTRODUCTION

This short survey offers a cross-section of the pottery made and marketed in and around the Mediterranean (the *mare nostrum* of the Romans) in ancient Roman times, here illustrated by some of the many items in the collections of the British Museum. While Roman wares from Britain and nearby are perhaps more familiar to many British visitors, and are the stuff of many museum displays, their mates from the provinces at the heart of the Roman Empire, including Rome itself, have often been less easy to visualise. The opening of the new Wolfson Gallery in the Museum now at last permits a full sampling of these Mediterranean wares to be viewed in one place. The Museum, by dint of its long history of collecting, is singularly well placed to illustrate the products of these other parts of the Roman Empire.[1]

For the better part of a century, Walters' *Catalogue*[2] has been a *vademecum* to those seeking information in English on Roman pottery from Britain and the Roman world at large. Since Walters' day, the study of Roman Britain and its neighbours in the Roman Empire – Gaul and the Rhineland – has made great progress, not least in the field of pottery research. Indeed, a specialist journal now exists for Romano-British pottery.[3] Until fairly recently, though, the study of Roman-period pottery in Mediterranean lands has lagged behind. For many years, it was treated in English-language circles (and, indeed, in its native regions) as the poor cousin of Greek vases, which were more suited to the dominant art-historical fashions in research. It is only since about 1970 that 'local' Roman archaeology in Mediterranean lands has adopted modern archaeological techniques and come to terms with the full range of its regional ceramic products, the result being a plethora of publications in numerous languages. The first sections of Walters' *Catalogue* thus still retain a good deal of value.

Some of the pots illustrated below appear in Walters' *Catalogue*; a few are listed in Dalton's *Catalogue of Early Christian Antiquities*; some of the Egyptian items are published in the relevant excavation reports, but others have hitherto escaped notice in print. I have tried here to present a series of new illustrations to supplement those already available elsewhere. The bibliography cited is perforce selective, with an emphasis on relevant recent studies.

For the sake of convenience, Roman pottery may here be defined

11

as that made and used within Italy and the Roman provinces between about 100 BC and AD 600, and its stylistic precursors and successors (which, in the East, lasted until the rise of Islam). In political terms, the history of Rome and its empire comprises the Republican period (*c.* 509–31 BC) and the Imperial period (31 or 27 BC–AD 324, 410 or 476, depending on which criteria are used). Culturally, it overlapped in its early years the end of the ancient Greek world – the 'Hellenistic' period – and, later on, the emergence of a new Christian 'Byzantine' civilisation centred on Constantinople. North of the Alps, the beginning and end of 'Roman' culture are conveniently marked by the conquest of the regions by Julius Caesar and his successors and then by their loss to Germanic invaders in the years after AD 400, both of which events led to marked changes in life-styles. In the Mediterranean, however, Rome took over from earlier civilisations, and the Byzantine and Islamic cultures which followed adopted many 'Roman' features. Hence what we term 'Roman' pottery cannot be bracketed within hard-and-fast dates. Its principal technical features – red (rather than black) glossy surfaces, the use of stamps and rouletting,[4] barbotine[5] and mould-formed applied ornament (pl. 1), manufacture within moulds or over forming devices – are in fact all in evidence by *c.* 200 BC somewhere in the Mediterranean world, whether in the 'Hellenistic' East or in Italy. Only the use of lead glazes (not particularly common and in any case intermittent) strikes a new note: see col. pl. V. In common with other craft products, the pottery of Roman times exhibits certain stylistic trends, some of Italian origin, others resulting from the exchange of ideas within a single vast economic system – the Empire. By later Imperial times (third–fourth centuries AD) various provincial centres, from Britain to Egypt, were purveying their own 'Roman' styles of pottery. Each of these was distinct, but all shared some common features.

Our knowledge of Roman pottery comes almost entirely from archaeological finds, especially the complete vessels found in graves and in ancient shipwrecks. Specific references to pots are rare in Roman literary texts and documents (a few can be gleaned from papyri), and types of Roman pots recognisable to an archaeologist do not often figure on Roman artwork such as sculpture, painting, or mosaic floors. The vessels depicted on the latter are either more up-market (silverware, for instance), or are conventional renderings of ancient forms like the Greek *krater*, or again are shown in very generalised – one might say 'cartoon' – form.

Various approaches can be taken to this abundant material, ranging from pure artistic appreciation to chemical analysis of the materials used and statistical study of trading patterns;[6] others may yet emerge. From an artistic standpoint, one cannot easily approach

Plate I Decorative treatments on Italian terra sigillata. Applied motifs. *Top*: plate, stamped by L. Gellius. Diam. 17.5 cm. *Left*: hand-rolled (?) applied spectacle spiral on plate. Barbotine ornament. *Bottom left*: dish, from Tharros. Diam. 16.5 cm. Rouletting. *Bottom right*: cup, from Tharros. Diam. 13.2 cm.

Roman pottery in the same way as one does earlier Greek 'vases', though the two are often related in terms of basic techniques. The Greek vessels are appreciated mainly for the motifs painted on them, which may reveal an individual artist's hand.[7] Roman pots, however – with some notable exceptions, mostly produced in the outer provinces – exhibit the potter's art, which may result in a pleasing combination of form with simple decorative effects, but rarely reveals the personal touch. A growing emphasis on quick production (always a matter of livelihood, for the lowly Mediterranean potter) is in evidence, with increased use of moulds to produce decoration mechanically. Where figured decoration is present, it tends to be in the form of cartoon-like individual renderings of well-known motifs (standard imagery of gods and heroes, for example) rather than co-ordinated scenes telling stories, such as one finds in Greek art. The exception to this can be seen on red-gloss Arretine ware and lead-glazed vessels of the time of the Emperor Augustus and his successors (*c.* 25 BC–AD 50). The delicate relief ornament on these vessels reflects the 'official' court aesthetic of the period, which recurs in a very wide range of other media (wall-painting, silverware, ivory-carving, coins, gem-engraving and so on).[8]

Roman pots, in common with Greek, also provide evidence for ancient literacy: makers' stamps and shipping instructions quite often appear on them, and pots (or broken fragments) can also serve as the medium for longer written texts (an example is the 'Aswan' dish noted below, pl. 2).[9]

DISTRIBUTION

A major feature of the Roman wares of the Mediterranean is the very wide distribution of a relatively small number of fine wares. As a result of easy sea links, the whole Mediterranean coastline served as a potential market, as it had done previously for Athenian products in the Classical Greek period of the fifth century BC. These wares – the Campana black-gloss wares of the Naples region and Etruria *c.* 200–50 BC, the Italian and Eastern Sigillata wares in the first and second centuries AD, and the African Red Slip wares and their derivatives thereafter – were particularly influential and were widely copied (pl. 14, fig. 3.3). Some pieces of the same fifth- and sixth-century Asia Minor and North African vessel-types found in excavations in Istanbul and at Tintagel in Cornwall (fig. 1.1) may serve as an illustration from later times. Some cooking wares (chiefly Italian and North African) were similarly traded.[10] Rarely, a fine-ware pot from far away may have inspired metalware, down to the maker's signature, as seems evidenced in Nubia (fig. 2 and pl. 16 *bottom* – possibly a local copy of Gaulish samian ware).

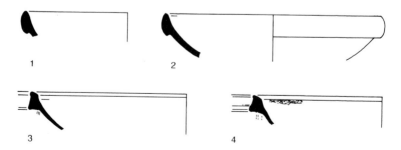

Figure I   Excavation finds from Tintagel (1, 3) and Istanbul, Great Palace (2, 4), compared. African and Phocean wares (scale 1:3).

Figure 2 Lathe-turned bronze bowl from Nubia (scale 1:3).

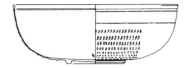

1

2

3

Figure 3 (1) Nabatean bowl from Petra, gift of Princess Michael of Kent (1977). (2, 3) Eastern copies of Italian cup-shapes: (2) from Knidos (Newton's excavations); (3) from Ephesus (Wood's excavations, 1864) (all scale 1:3).

IDENTIFICATION OF SOURCES

In contrast to the situation in Roman Britain and Gaul, the production centres of Roman Mediterranean wares are very patchily documented, as is also the case with their Greek and Italic precursors. Where kiln-sites are known, they are rarely recorded in detail. Among the workshops producing red-gloss and red-slip wares, those making Arretine ware are documented by quantities of waste products (chiefly mould fragments, pl. 4), mostly recovered a century ago. The workshops of Pergamon are well recorded in Loeschcke's work carried out over eighty years ago at Çandarlı, and by more recent finds. Most other Eastern Sigillata production centres are not even known. Some of the African centres have been located, but only one or two have been properly investigated. Little is known of the factories for lead-glazed and relief wares. The production centres of amphorae are beginning to be documented, but literally hundreds remain to be pin-pointed. Ancient literary and documentary sources do exist, but they are scattered. They include, notably, a brief mention of production centres by Pliny the Elder,[11] an Egyptian papyrus with details of a leasing arrangement for the making of pots (mostly amphorae related to pl. 9 *right*)[12] and that quoted on p. 27. Stamps on fine-ware vessels and especially on commercial amphorae, together with producers' and shippers' markings on the

15

Plate 2 Red-slipped Aswan-ware bowl, c. AD 600–750 (scale c. 2:3).

latter (such as inked or painted inscriptions and stamped stoppers) may provide more information on both sources and original contents. In contrast, those on bulky storage-jars (*dolia*), which are common in Italy, often indicate the owners of workshops as much as their physical locations, since in this case it is the potters, rather than their pots, who may have moved around. Quite unusual is the late bowl (pl. 2) of Egyptian Red Slip A ware. This ware is generally assigned an Aswan source, here proved by an ink inscription in Coptic, translatable as 'the plate [*pinax* – a Greek word] of Souan'. This bowl was found downstream at Nagada near Luxor, hence the

Plate 3 Mouldmade lamp, of Pisidian (Asia Minor) type, but of Egyptian (western Nile Delta) manufacture of high quality. Advertised on the bottom as 'Sagalassikon' = '[product] of Sagalassos', probably early 2nd century AD. Length 7.8 cm, width 6.5 cm.

I Amphora, Cilician (or Cypriot?), 'Late Roman type I', with red paint label (*dipinto*). Found in Egypt, late 4th or 5th century AD. Height 50.0 cm.

II *Above*: Red-gloss wares from Italian and Asia Minor workshops. *Left*: beaker with appliqués, Pergamon, c. 100–50 BC. *Front left*: small bowl, Italian, stamped INAC / HVS, c. AD 1–30. *Top centre*: relief-ware chalice (foot restored), Arretine, c. 25–1 BC. *Front right*: beaker, signed L.SARIVS.L.L.SVRVS, c. AD 1–30. *Right*: platter, Arretine ware, stamped CN ATEI, c. 10 BC–AD10. Diam. 32.7 cm.

III *Left*: Painted jar, Egyptian, c. 2nd century AD.

IV Thin-walled decorated wares made in the Aswan region, Upper (southern) Egypt, with barbotine or two-tone painted decoration (scale c. 1:3). *Left to right*: two-handled jar with attached lid, painted leaf-sprays (black) and bands (red); shallow cup with painted Nubian (black) on interior; two-handled jar with two-colour barbotine ornament. All late 1st or 2nd century AD.

V Lead-glazed cups, early to mid-1st century AD. *Left*: probably South Italian, found at Kouklia (Old Paphos), Cyprus. *Right*: Mytilene product, with white clay inserts under the glaze. Diam. (rim) 9.5 cm; (with handles) 15.2 cm. Height 7.6 cm.

VI Two small containers, for perfumes or medications, Nile Delta, perhaps 2nd century AD. *Left*: bust (bottom missing) of Hermes with lotus leaf flanked by wings on brow. Height 9.6 cm. *Right*: head of man, bald. Height 8.6 cm.

VII Plate with serving compartments (small inset bowls), Aswan (Egyptian) ware, copying African Red Slip ware. Pink clay, yellow slip with black painting, c. 7th century AD. Diam. (rim) 33 cm. Height 5.4 cm.

need for a label. Stamps may, however, give unreliable sources – for example, the 'Arretina' stamps on some eastern finds usually advertise 'Arretine-type' products made locally, rather than the genuine article. The clay lamp (pl. 3) which calls itself a '[product] of Sagalassos' (a fine-ware production centre in Asia Minor) was actually made in Egypt, in the western Nile Delta – presumably in a new workshop staffed by foreign craftsmen intent on advertising their wares.

FUNCTIONS AND SHAPES

In Mediterranean lands, where wheelmade pottery had been the norm for centuries, if not millennia, the role of pottery vessels as containers either for on-site storage or for shipping, as cheap – rather than luxury – kitchen- and tablewares, as burial urns and offerings in graves, was well established. These basic functions altered little during Roman times, though some differences in emphasis may be seen. Changes in burial practices led to an increased use of glass vessels and clay lamps at the expense of pottery vessels, and eventually, under Christian influence, to the abandonment of all grave offerings, though this was not uniform in all areas. Glass vessels came to challenge pots as cheap drinking vessels and containers for liquids, to the extent that some pottery vessels copied glassware shapes. The cheap pottery perfume flasks (*unguentaria*) which were often placed in graves in Hellenistic times had been effectively ousted by glass versions by AD 100. A fashion for glass burial urns is also to be noted.

Less common functions for pottery vessels may be observed, including use as clay beehives, lanterns, and hot-water compresses for medical purposes. Some of these originated in pre-Roman times; the three examples cited are commonest in the Roman period, though only in certain regions. Some pots were frankly made as souvenirs, with inscriptions on them referring to spectator sports. (The pot itself was not the prize, as the Greek Panathenaic vases had been.)

Roman (and also Jewish) culinary practices demanded specific vessel-shapes, examples of this being the flat baking pans (*patinae*) and baking covers noted below (p.78). However, the traditional heavy grinding basins for kitchen use (*mortaria*, fig. 34) were now often replaced by stone versions. Common Mediterranean practice here diverged from that in the northern Roman provinces, as did preferences for drinking vessels with or without handles. Further comments on these points are made in the text below (pp. 78–80).

The shapes of Mediterranean Roman pottery, particularly the

tablewares, constantly imitate metalware of their own and occasionally earlier times (see pl. 13). This reflects the natural desire of the consumer to go up-market – silverware was, after all, the basic Roman status symbol. One example of this is the flat platters noted below (pp. 20–1, see figs. 14, 18), which were difficult to make.

PRODUCTION

Most Roman pots were simply thrown on a potter's wheel and then cut off the still-rotating wheel with a wire or string, leaving the typical 'fingerprint' marks on the bottom. A neater base (or low foot) was then normally produced by inverting the vessel, half-dried, on the wheel and shaving off excess clay as both revolved. Marks of this turning process are often visible on the finished vessel in the form of horizontal scratches and spatula-marks (see fig. 3 *centre*, pl. 2 and others). Necks and feet might be formed as separate elements and be added afterwards – slight bulges, seam-lines or rough edges on interiors may be evidence of this. The *costrel* shape, particularly common in Egypt and Palestine, comprises two wheelmade elements for the closed body and a third for a neck attached at the side (fig. 4.3, cf. fig. 25.9), to which handles may be added by hand. Large tall vessels such as the commercial wine-amphorae tended to be assembled from three or more wheel-thrown sections, the joins being smoothed over before the firing. An Egyptian jug (fig. 4.1) is unusual in having a body formed of two pieces which had been rotated in different directions on the wheel, as is clear from the ribbed treatment visible on them.

The finer Roman wares are generally more thinly potted and delicately finished than modern craft pottery (see especially fig. 27). The basic methods of production can hardly have differed much from those used by earlier Greek and Near Eastern potters. Indeed, almost identical pots (often ribbed in the Roman manner) are known from Syria and Mesopotamia over two thousand years earlier. However, a significant proportion of Roman vessels were formed within a mould mounted upon the potter's wheel; elements such as rims might protrude above the encasing mould, and feet and handles, formed separately, might be added after the initial forming. Sigillata ware bowls with relief decoration were made thus (col. pl. II *top centre*, and fig. 5), and a good number of broken pieces of the actual moulds from the Arretine workshops (pl. 4, and fig. 5) can be studied at the British Museum. These take the form of thick-walled bowls in smooth hard-fired reddish ware. Punches (usually referred to by the French term *poinçons*) were used to impress the individual motifs on their smooth inner surfaces. The same method

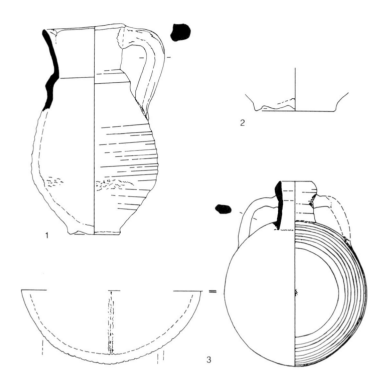

Figure 4 Techniques of manufacture: wares from Egypt (scale 1:3).

of manufacture is seen among lead-glazed wares. In other instances, individual motifs made in moulds were applied to the surface of a wheelmade pot (see the beaker in col. pl. II).

In fact, the old finds still tell us very little in detail about the production techniques of the potters of Arezzo, except by analogy with their successors in Gaul. For many undecorated vessels also, production aided by moulds is probable, though difficult to prove. Earlier generations of archaeologists may simply have overlooked the presence of plain moulds, especially if broken or made of perishable materials like plaster.

In the mass-produced sigillata wares of Italy and the Levant we meet footed plates with wide horizontal floors, from which variously profiled rims rise at the outer edge (figs. 14, 18). Some of these 'platters' measure 60 cm or more in diameter and some form of

Plate 4 Mould *right* for the production of Arretine relief ware and *left* modern cast (scale 1:3).

support must have been needed to prevent sagging and deformation of the still-wet clay during their manufacture. Two possible ways, involving moulds, for Eastern Sigillata A and for Italian (Arretine) Sigillata respectively, are illustrated in figs. 6 and 7. In both instances one surface of the resulting pot is completely smooth, while the other (that presumed to have been exposed during manufacture) displays slight brush-marks. The gentle sagging of the heavy rim of

Figure 5 Cross-section of the mould above (pl. 4), and reconstruction of the type of vessel produced from it (scale 1:3).

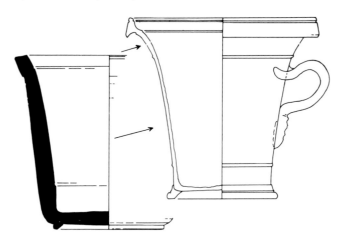

the Arretine example (which is quite often observed) presumably occurred at a late stage, after the plate had been turned the right way up in order to receive the potter's stamp. Slight traces of stacking are seen at the bases of the feet and on the floors immediately above them, showing how such vessels were positioned for firing. Note the imprints of three rectangular support-pads seen in col. pl. II and pl. 5. These seem to have been coated with fine sand or the like to prevent the clay of the pad from fusing with that of the plate during the firing. The marks of such pads are especially common on the heavy dishes produced at Çandarlı (Pergamon). Particularly elaborate stacking arrangements were needed for early Roman lead-glazed wares (see pp. 64–5).

As in Hellenistic times, many vessels, including some of the fine wares, bear a slip on the more visible parts only (i.e. the outside or

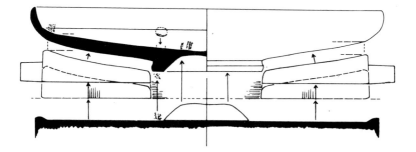

Figure 6 Eastern Sigillata A ware plate: probable technique of manufacture (scale 1:3).

Figure 7 Italian terra sigillata plate: technique of manufacture (scale 1:3).

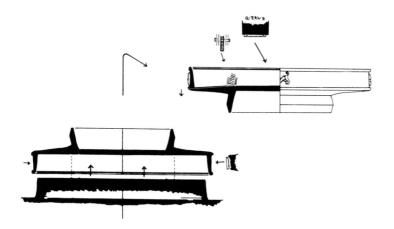

Plate 5 Production defects. *Top*: floor of Arretine platter (see col. pl. II), showing the imprints of pads (sanded, to avoid fusion) from stacking for firing. Stamp of Cn. Ateius, with letters combined, and palm-branch ornament (scale 2:3). *Left*: jug, dented in the kiln, from Kerch, Crimea. Local early Roman product. Height 15.9 cm.

top), the result of a quick partial immersion in a clay solution; smudges (here visible on pl. 5 *left* and pl. 14 *right*) often appear around or above the base to show where the vessel was grasped for this purpose. On several Eastern fine wares (see below) one can observe a transverse streak of slightly darker colour where two partial applications of slip overlap. This 'double-dipping streak' is already seen on some second-century BC black-gloss products from Greece (pl. 6) including Corinthian relief-ware 'Megarian' bowls.

The application of the glaze material on the lead-glazed wares seems not to have been uniform. Some vessels bear the scars of a tripod stilt arrangement used to separate them in the kiln. Some were clearly fired upside-down, since 'drops' of glaze have formed on the rim, creating pronounced knobs (see fig. 26); on others the glaze is of uniform thickness. Some recent finds of kiln-furniture and debris from Perge in southern Turkey – now seen to have been a significant production centre in the period from Augustus to Claudius – help to clarify this picture. The stacking arrangements for the kilns evidenced there are in fact quite complicated.

It seems likely that some of the larger African Red Slip products were made in plaster/stucco moulds (just like contemporary lamps), though at present the only definite evidence of this is for vessels which were clearly not formed on a wheel, such as rectangular trays. Many Italian thin-walled bowls and beakers of early Imperial date, and not just those bearing relief patterns (col. pl. II *front right*, and fig. 15.2), may also have been made thus. It is difficult to imagine how eggshell-thin vessels of the type of fig. 27.2 could have been made in quantity (as they evidently were) without some moulding process. The careful turning required to produce their smooth exteriors would otherwise have been very risky, and would have slowed down production to a point that was surely

Plate 6 Black-gloss medallion bowl, showing 'double-dipping streak'. Diam. 16.2 cm.

uneconomic. Partial moulds seem also to have been used in the production of large flat baking pans – notably the classic varieties of Pompeian Red ware (fig. 32) – some of which are stamped or signed in relief on their bottoms.

Some other wares, both fine and coarse, were made in the manner of figurines and lamps, by pressing clay into two or more moulds of various shapes, and by assembling the impressions into hollow vessels. In this way closed shapes (jugs, bottles and so on) and vases in the form of figurines could be produced: examples here are the Knidian series (pl. 26) and the figurine vases (col. pl. VI).

A feature of the sigillata wares and the African Red Slip wares noted below (p. 59) is the uniformity of their firing, which entailed (at least on some series) the use of a special flue system in the kiln. Among the coarser wares, certain peculiarities serve to identify Roman-period wares over large parts of the Mediterranean:

1. Ribbing or wheel-ridging of the body, particularly on closed shapes and on cooking vessels. The latter (seen also on certain earlier Egyptian and Syrian wares) seems to start on Palestinian and Syrian (?) cooking wares as early as c. 150 BC, but is not common there and in Egypt until the first century AD (fig. 33, pl. 7). In the Aegean and central Mediterranean areas it becomes common during the second and third centuries (fig. 31.5–7).

2. Indented bases with an inset 'button' at the centre (fig. 4 *top right*). This seems to be a manufacturing trick, either to ensure proper centring of the ball of raw clay on the wheel, or to form the closure of an element thrown upside-down. It is seen on some Levantine wares of later Hellenistic times and is widespread thereafter, occurring from Sardinia to Palestine.

3. Sliced handles formed of a strip with one edge sliced off straight with a knife, instead of being tapered or rounded off in the normal manner. These are found occasionally in Cyprus as early as the first century BC and are a feature of Aegean cooking pots from the first century AD. Thereafter they are common on closed vessels and cooking pots in other regions (figs. 4.1, 31.5 and pl. 7). Such handles are not generally noted on ancient wares of other periods.

Evidence for the production of cooking and domestic ware can also be gleaned from Jewish (Talmudic) texts. In particular, a type of casserole with close-fitting lid (p.80) may be identified there.

Some production faults can be seen on the pots illustrated here. A jug from Kerch (pl. 5 *left*) has a deep gash on the body which may have been inflicted just prior to firing. Often, firing is uneven, resulting in differences in colour from one part of a vessel to another, depending on the way that the vessels were stacked, i.e., whether

Plate 7 Three pots (made in Egypt) showing typical Roman treatments: ribbing, 'sliced' handles, rouletting. Height 22.2, 20.9, 17.0 cm.

the surface was exposed to changes in the kiln atmosphere during firing. Sometimes, especially on thin-walled beakers and mugs, this was exploited to produce a two-tone effect (figs. 27.3, 28 *right*, and pls. 24 *top*, 25 *right*).

SIZES

It was noted long ago that certain fine-ware shapes tend to recur in more or less uniform sizes. This observation was reinforced by the discovery of tally-lists from the South Gaulish Sigillata production sites noting specific sizes. While these sizes cannot in practice have been applied industry-wide and at all times, a standard plate-size (*c.* 16–18 cm diameter, for individual servings) and two sizes of open cups and bowls (*c.* 11–14 cm and 6–8 cm) do recur among the Italian and Gaulish Sigillata wares of around the first century AD (fig. 14), and these are more or less adopted on the imitations made in Eastern factories (as in fig. 20). A series of larger plates ('platters'), with different treatment of the foot, occurs in matching forms, but these do not exhibit standard dimensions. The smaller plate-size is matched, at first, in the African series (fig. 22.1–4), but the later dishes and plates are larger, reproducing the sizes of contemporary metalware (fig. 22.7, 10), and cups are few.

A counter tendency, with commercial advantages, may already have developed in Asia Minor in the first century. Some finds from

25

shipwrecks suggest that some early fine wares from here were made in several graded sizes, which could be more closely packed for shipping than the Italian vessels with their awkwardly projecting feet. Different considerations applied in the case of shipping containers such as amphorae. While these vessels were made as far as possible to a uniform size within each workshop (a difficult aim with handmade products), indications of the actual contents tended to be scratched or painted on after filling; most are in cryptic abbreviated form (col. pl. I, pl. 10 *left*). In any case, amphora sizes varied greatly from region to region, and from century to century – the *caveat emptor* rule applied here.

QUANTITIES

Mediterranean sites tend to produce far more pottery finds than those in, say, Britain. A Roman-period urban Mediterranean site may yield over a million sherds per hectare; a medium-sized excavation can come up with 100,000 or more during a season. The chief reason for this is the very widespread use of clay amphorae as shipping containers. Shipwrecks have produced them by the thousand, and on the average urban excavation site amphora sherds comprise between about 50 and 85 per cent of all pottery found, while fine tablewares constitute *c.* 10 per cent or less. Hence, while the finer wares may have been used in similar quantities, on Mediterranean sites they are only about a third as common in relative terms as in Britain.

Amphorae

[Received:] 2 *maurai*, 3 *hadrianai*, 1 *lagoinos*, . . . *kretika*, 3 *knidia*, . . . *dichora*, 4(?) *aminnaiai* (i.e. Mauretanian and northern Adriatic [jars], 'wine-jar', Cretan and Knidian, [local] double-sizers, Campanian)

From a papyrus management account from the Fayum, Egypt, dated to the period AD 249–68, quoted by D. Rathbone in *Economic Rationalism and Rural Society in Third-Century AD Egypt* (Cambridge 1991: 304). He further comments, 'When . . . received . . . , they probably no longer contained wine from their areas of production, but had been reused.'

The normal commercial container for liquid (and sometimes dry) goods in Mediterranean lands was a two-handled jar of elongated or rounded form, the *amphora*,[13] which also gave its name to a Roman measure of capacity.[14] The shape, originally bullet-shaped with small handles on the body – a type which survived into Roman times in the Punic domains of North Africa – was adopted by the Greeks around 700 BC; Greek versions have a neck, often long, flanked by handles. Designed for stowing on board ships, they taper to a projecting solid toe, which aided handling and reduced the chance of breakage. Roman examples, identifiable from *c.* 250 BC onwards, generally follow the Greek pattern. A yellowish or light brown coloration, at least on the surface, was generally preferred in Hellenistic and Roman times.

Most complete surviving ancient amphorae come from shipwrecks, of which hundreds are now documented from the Mediterranean.[15] Another rich source is burials, particularly in fringe regions like Gaul, Britain and Nubia – regions where the contents of the amphorae, not being locally produced, might rate as a luxury. Wine and olive-oil were the chief contents; pickled fish-sauce (*garum*) and various dry goods were also shipped in them.

The shapes of Roman amphorae (like those of modern bottles) served to a certain extent to identify the type of contents and not only regional origins. Most distinctive are the heavy globular olive-oil amphorae from southern Spain (pl. 8 *right* shows a late version)

Plate 8 *Left*: Palestinian ring-handled amphora, LR Amphora Carthage 5 = Benghazi LR 4 (cf. Peacock class 46), 6th–7th century AD. *Right*: Spanish baggy oil-amphora, Dressel 23 (derivative of Dressel 20), c. late 3rd–4th century AD.

and the tall, extremely heavy wine-amphorae of the first century BC from Etruria and central Italy (fig. 8.1). Both of these, the products of highly commercialised systems, normally have producers' stamps in Latin on their handles.[16] Stamps are also present on some other Roman amphorae (see fig. 9 for a selection). Alternative means of identification were stamps on the stoppers, although these are not often found (pl. 10 *right*) and markings inscribed or scrawled in paint or ink directly onto the vessel, indicating contents, shipper, recipient and so on (col. pl. I).[17]

Hundreds of different varieties of amphorae were produced in Roman times, some of which are found throughout the Empire. The shapes found in Rome were classified a century ago by Dressel, whose typology is still much cited.[18] A recent reclassification in English is that of Peacock and Williams;[19] this adds the results of petrographic analysis of the grits in the clay of the pots, permitting more precise pin-pointing of their source areas, in cases where makers' stamps and documented kiln-sites are lacking.

In the later Republican period (late third to mid-first century BC), three large regional series of amphorae typified the products of Roman-ruled Italy. All to a certain extent follow the 'Greek' (Hellenistic) trends seen elsewhere in this period: long necks, pointed toes, handles bearing name-stamps, a pale surface colour

28

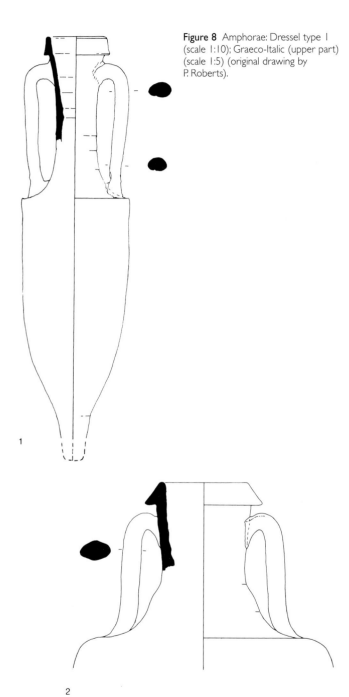

Figure 8 Amphorae: Dressel type 1 (scale 1:10); Graeco-Italic (upper part) (scale 1:5) (original drawing by P. Roberts).

1

2

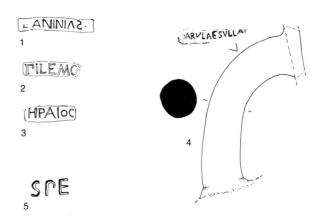

Figure 9 Amphora stamps (scale 1:3). (1–3) Brindisi type, late 2nd–1st century BC.
(4) Adriatic Italy? 2nd–1st century BC? (5) Northern Adriatic, 1st–2nd century AD.
(6–7) Unknown variant of North African.
(8–10) Finds from the Monte Testaccio, Rome: (8) Lusitanian, mid-3rd century AD, and
(9, 10) South Spanish, 2nd–3rd century AD.

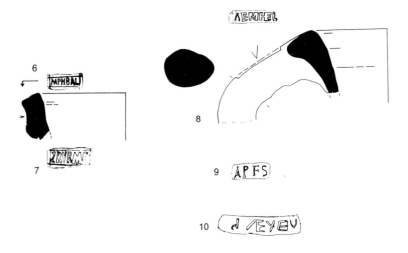

and so on. In southern Italy – the area known as Magna Graecia and including the Naples region – a version with a pear-shaped body and overhanging triangular rim (see fig. 8.2) was current around 250–100 BC. This is commonly known as 'Graeco-Italic', on account of its strongly Greek features. Rather later, an unusually large and cumbersome type (Dressel type 1; fig. 8), with thick walls and elongated neck and handles, appeared up the western, Tyrrhenian, coast, from northern Campania to Etruria. Many examples of these amphorae, widely exported around the western Mediterranean, bear stamps showing that they come from the estates of the aristocracy. The names include those of Roman senators, who were at the time officially banned from commercial profiteering – the amphorae paint another picture! The vintage Falernian and Caecuban wines mentioned by Roman writers and poets travelled mostly in such jars. A third major series, more round-bodied and fairly short-necked, is seen in the Adriatic region from about 130 BC onward. Early production sites for these are known near Brindisi. The amphorae from here bear stamps on their handles either in Latin or Greek (see fig. 9). Later, heavier thick-walled versions of these (Lamboglia type 2), probably influenced by the Tyrrhenian series, were made further north (at Issa in the middle of the Adriatic, for example). These, in turn, gave rise to a baggy type (Dressel 6), bearing large rim-stamps in Latin, made in the Veneto and Istria (northern Adriatic) from the time of Augustus onward. Like the heavy globular Spanish amphorae, these may mostly have been containers for olive-oil.

In the Roman Imperial period (c. 30–20 BC onwards), the shapes of amphorae become more indicative of contents than, as in the earlier Greek manner, of region of production. For instance, the shape of Hellenistic amphorae from Kos was adopted in Augustan times in Italy as the standard wine-container (Dressel types 2–4; cf. pl. 9 *left*). The shape was then copied in various other parts of the Roman Empire, even (though rarely) as far afield as Britain.[20] Other Greek-derived amphorae from Italy and the East – some elongated, some smaller and round-bottomed – are mostly quite thin-walled and light-weight in relation to their contents; the Greek term *kouphon*, known from papyrus records, appears to denote these. A baggy hollow-toed type, with long handles set very close to the neck, was adopted in Spain for *garum* (fish-sauce) containers.

A selection of first- to fourth-century types and of the stamps found on them is shown in figs. 8, 10 and pls. 8–9. In the first century AD a clear distinction can usually be made between large bulk-transport amphorae and smaller flat-based amphora-flagons for use at table (see pl. 9 *left* from Pompeii, for an example of the latter). Thereafter, the differences in size and shape become more blurred.

Plate 9 *Left*: Pompeii table-amphora, variant of Dressel 2–4 (scale c. 1:5). *Right*: Romano-Egyptian amphora, made of brown Nile silt. 'Hermopolis' version (ribbed all over), perhaps an example of the 'double-size' (*dichoron*) shape mentioned in papyrus texts. Found at Tanis (?), 1st–2nd century AD. Height 96.5 cm.

Rather small amphorae, lacking stamps, are common in many parts of Italy, Greece and elsewhere in the second to fourth centuries AD. An early hybrid version made in the Marseille region is seen in fig. 10.1, a find from the Rhineland.

Some small amphorae were used for other commodities. Tiny carrot-shaped vessels with small handle-rings on the body, made in Berytus (Beirut) and elsewhere, are known to have contained dates and other such goods. A somewhat similar type made on the island of Lipari (southern Italy) may have been used for shipping alum.[21]

After c. AD 400 much of this diversity disappears, to be superseded by the products of a few large (possibly officially sponsored)

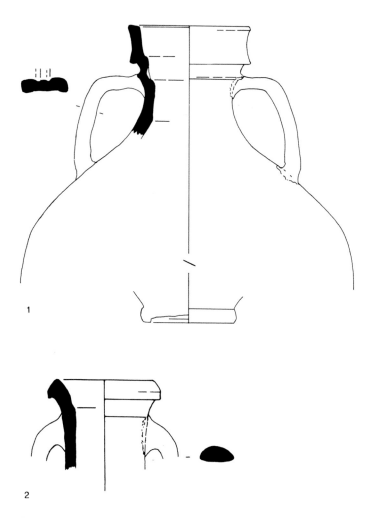

Figure 10 Amphorae (scale 1:4), (1) Marseille type ('Gauloise 2'), about 25 BC–AD 15, found in the Rhineland. (2) *Spatheion* rim (detail; see pl. 38 *left*).

centres. Noteworthy among these are buff-ware examples from Cilicia (col. pl. I), late versions of the traditional Palestinian shape from Gaza and the Negev (pl. 8 *left*) and Egyptian products (pl. 9 *right*), among others. Long cylindrical amphorae with short necks, in reddish fabrics, often with a distinctive pale outer surface due to an application of salt water, are the typical North African olive-oil containers of *c.* AD 200–600. A slender carrot-shaped version of the

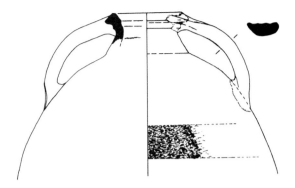

Figure 11 Egyptian amphora, from excavations at Tanis, 1st–2nd century AD (scale 1:6).

latter, the so-called *spatheion* ('sword-shaped [jar]': see pl. 10 *left*, and pl. 38 *left* with detail fig. 10.2), which was common in the fifth and sixth centuries, may have contained wine or some other product. These Late Roman shapes are scarcely ever stamped, but many bear scrawled ink markings, either indications of contents and so on, or protective symbols such as crosses.

While the original contents of these vessels have almost always vanished, a resinous coating (generally seen as a blackish stain) may survive on the inner surface, indicating that this was how seepage was prevented. Such staining is common on a long-lived series of slender micaceous brown jars from Asia Minor, perhaps the 'Tmolan

Plate 10 *Left*: amphora neck with original plaster seal in place, North African carrot-shaped (*spatheion*) type (made in Tunisia?). Red paint indication of capacity (?) in Greek letters (XMG), 5th–6th century (scale 2:5). *Right*: amphora stopper with relief letters. Northern Adriatic? Found in Malta, 1st century BC or AD. Diam. 8.2 cm.

Figure 12 (1) Amphora stopper? and (2) flagon stopper, with slip on upper part, 1st–2nd century AD (scale 1:3).

jars' of the papyri, and the late Gaza products, among others. Discarded amphorae could be used in various ways, most commonly as makeshift coffins for burials (which they may help to date).

The essential stoppers and seals of ancient amphorae are mostly lost, except for a number of finds from shipwrecks and some from desert sites. Materials used for these included plaster or stucco, volcanic ash, wood and cork, sometimes sealed in place with another material. Impressed, relief or branded stamps are occasionally present on them, giving producers' or shippers' names. A series of clay disks with rough relief lettering or patterns (pl. 10 *right*) appears to match the Adriatic Italian amphora series of *c.* 100 BC–AD 100, but otherwise clay lids are abnormal. Some late amphora seals bear Christian motifs: see the plaster example (pl. 10 *left*) on a late North African product found in Egypt. String-holes on the latter show how the stopper was removed. An earlier series of small vases with sharply splayed rims (fig. 12.1) may have had a similar function – set upside-down in a plaster seal to serve as a bung, the vase would have been wrenched out to break the seal, which explains why almost all such finds lack their rims.

DOLIA

Large thick-walled clay jars (Latin *dolium*, Greek *pithos*) were manufactured for on-site bulk storage of liquids either on the farm where the goods were produced or at the retail end of the process. Roman examples from Italy, produced in sections or built up from coils, mostly have a heavy wheel-turned rim, and often bear a large maker's stamp on the rim or shoulder similar to those found on stamped bricks and *mortaria* (cf. pl. 32 *bottom*). Those from the eastern provinces illustrate traditional types and are rarely stamped. They are generally little studied.

FINE WARES

FORERUNNERS

The finer pottery of Rome and of its surroundings (Latium, Etruria) in the later Republican period is best seen as part of a larger Mediterranean picture. Fine black-gloss wares in the Greek tradition were dominant after about 400 BC, and in Etruria and Campania one sees the end of the painted Greek vase tradition. Then, while these Greek-derived wares were in decline in southern – Greek colonial – Italy during the third century, practically disappearing there after the Second Punic War (218–201 BC), new versions appeared in the Roman core area, normally bearing stamps rather than painting. Some have glossy black-slip surfaces, quite the equal of those typifying the best Greek wares, and may have been fired by the complicated process used for Greek painted vases. A simpler process, analogous to that used for some later Roman 'colour-coated' wares, was probably used for the more mediocre classes.

One workshop in the vicinity of Rome, known to scholars as the *atelier des petites estampilles* (pl. 11 top), produced Rome's first 'export' ware (c. 300–250 BC): fine-ware bowls (*pocula*) with small stamps, often apparently impressed from signet-rings. Similar bowls were made during the third century in other Italian centres; a few have figures painted in white over the black surface. Two or three generations later, products from Rome are represented by another series of bowls with gem-impressions of Hercules (*Heraklesschalen*: pl. 11 left). Plainer black-slipped vessels made in several local potteries served as the normal tablewares for the growing city.[22]

Late derivatives of the third-century types, in a heavy, roughly finished, purplish-red ware with a very hard metallic gloss, were produced in and around Naples. This so-called Campana A ware, made in great numbers in the period c. 200–50 BC, is a typical find on Roman Republican sites all over the western Mediterranean. Examples are much rarer in the East, though a fair number are seen at Delos. Its stamps, which date to the second century, and painted white bands hark back to earlier Greek models. Contrasting with this are some much finer wares from the former Etruscan region, which herald the classic Arretine ware of later times. One, the buff-bodied Campana B, made mostly after the mid-second century, bears very delicate rouletted bands and some stamps, normally

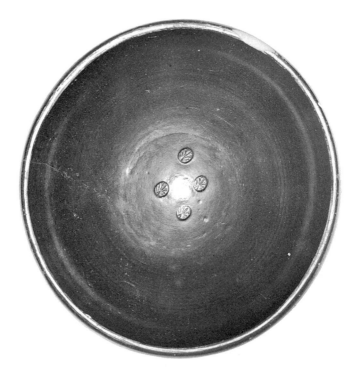

Plate 11 *Above: poculum* (drinking? bowl), with multiple stamps, from the *atelier des petites estampilles, c.* 300–260 BC (scale *c.* 2:3). *Left:* 'Hercules' dish, so named from the signet impression at its centre, *c.* 200 BC (scale *c.* 1:2).

confined between grooves – features shared with the later red Arretine wares. This ware introduces the large flat-floored plate as a common shape (compare the strangely similar Eastern Sigillata A ware type noted below, p. 57). A black gloss remains normal on this ware, though a whole or partial red firing marks off some of its local competitors. By 50 BC these wares were generally in decline; the transition to their red-gloss successors in the region remains patchily understood. Some of the later examples acquire potters' stamps.

In the first century BC, a series of reduction-fired grey-bodied wares appears in certain regions. These, requiring a simpler firing process, form a prelude to the red-bodied wares of the Imperial period. Best known and perhaps most widely distributed are the soft, somewhat micaceous Campana C wares of Sicily, consisting largely of flattish plates; their eastern counterparts are a series of large mould-formed platters with a polished black slip produced somewhere in the region of Ephesos in Asia Minor. Regional grey wares of significance are those from Metapontum (southern Italy) and Knidos, and an early series of Arezzo products ('Black Arretine') is also present. At least some of these survive throughout Augustan times. The unique grey-bodied vase in pl. 12 seems to be related to them.

Plate 12 A rare funerary vase (burial urn), in black Arretine (?) relief ware, with gold-leaf additions, c. 25–1 BC (scale 3:10).

Plate 13
Top: mouldmade
relief bowl, by
Popilius. Plain
ware without
slip, partly
blackened
where exposed
during the firing.
Made in Etruria,
c. 150 BC (scale
c. 1:2).
Bottom: silver
relief bowl,
found in
Bulgaria,
c. 200–150 BC.
Diam. 15.0 cm,
height 8.4 cm.

The relief-ware ('Megarian') bowls characteristic of the Hellenistic East[23] continued to be made there for a while under Roman rule. The Ephesos region (Asia Minor) was a major centre for these in the decades around 100 BC, and may have enjoyed certain trading privileges – its products are extremely common in the Roman *entrepôt* of Delos and occur sporadically in Italy, while a few even reached Spain. Some of the Ephesian bowls are fired grey; other grey-bodied versions are seen at Metapontum and in the crude 'Liburnian' class from Dalmatia. Such relief bowls were not often actually made in central and northern Italy, though some small classes in a thin uncoated fabric (matching that of the 'thin-walled' wares, p. 67) may be observed (pl. 13 *top*). Some of these are signed with 'Roman' names. They seem too early (perhaps *c.* 150–75 BC)²⁴ to have directly influenced the classic relief wares described below.

At Pergamon in Asia Minor the transition from earlier Greek to Roman wares is marked by a class of drinking vessels with applied plaques, impressed from moulds, most commonly bearing ivy motifs (col. pl. II *left*) or erotic encounters. These pots are often fired black or dark brown on the outside and a sigillata-red on the inside and around the base (implying firing in stacks). A parallel series shows wispy incised leaves and flowers enlivened with dots of white paint (a late version of the Hellenistic 'West Slope' decorative style). The kilns for these two series, which more or less span the first century BC, have been located at Pergamon-Kestel. Their 'waxy' gloss appearance is not matched on the later Pergamon sigillata wares, which were presumably produced in other workshops. Some imitations of the Pergamon shapes and applied ornaments are seen at Knidos, perhaps at Ephesos, and in southern Italy/Sicily in the region of the Straits of Messina.

Red-gloss sigillata wares

The typical Roman fine wares are those with a glossy red surface – a category known to modern scholars as *terra sigillata* or *samian* ware, both somewhat unsatisfactory terms, but ones made familiar by long usage.

The chief categories of these are the various Italian Sigillata wares, those from South Gaul and Spain, and some five major Eastern Sigillata wares (see below, pp. 53–4). (The Central and Eastern Gaulish wares found in Britain scarcely reached Mediterranean customers.) Any Mediterranean excavation site is liable to reveal examples of some or most of these 'import' wares (pl. 14), and local imitations of them are scarcer than on the land-locked sites of the northern Empire. A vivid example of the circulation of these wares is provided by a crateful of Gaulish wares from the south of France still not unpacked after shipping, found in the ruins of Pompeii.²⁵

Italian and western terra sigillata

Around 40 BC a fine-quality red ware with a glossy red-slipped surface began to be made at Arretium (modern Arezzo) in northern Tuscany, where some black-gloss wares had previously been produced. This 'Arretine' ware (some early versions are shown in fig. 13) developed rapidly into one of the flag-bearers of the regenerated Roman international culture of the age of Augustus, and,

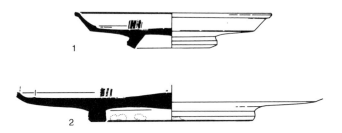

Figure 13 Italian terra sigillata, early products with multiple stamps (scale 1:3).
(1) Plate (*Conspectus* form 2), with stamps A.TITI / FIGVL[i] (see pl. 38 *bottom*).
(2) Base of platter, stamps L.VMBR[icii] / SEXTIO (see pl. 18.1).

within pottery-using circles, became enormously influential, especially in the newly acquired northern provinces of the expanding Roman Empire, like Gaul. Vessels bearing relief decoration, produced within moulds (such as pl. 4), were soon added to the ware's repertoire; these, along with some other features, betray Hellenistic Greek influence. The delicacy of the decoration and sharp angles of the developed forms ape contemporary metalware, especially silver plate. In general, sigillata shapes tend not to repeat those of contemporary glassware and the 'thin-walled' wares noted below (pp. 67–70). Vessel-shapes are distinctive and standardised, and a potter's name-stamp is almost always impressed on the floor (pl. 18.1, 3–6) or sometimes, rather incongruously, appears as a feature of the relief decoration (pl. 18.2).

Arretine ware is mentioned in ancient texts, and as a result of discoveries of the debris of several workshops at Arezzo, mainly during the later nineteenth century, the term became – in the predominantly northern European scholarly literature – almost synonymous with Italian Sigillata wares in general. Attention at that time was mainly focused on the relief-decorated wares, which appealed to contemporary Victorian taste, to the extent that a good many copies were produced, reconstituted from fragmentary ancient moulds or vessels (such as pl. 4). These, especially the complete 'moulds', may display slight 'seams' where breaks occurred on the original elements. The works of the German scholars Dragendorff, Loeschcke and Oxé (see bibliography), which not only detail the decorative styles but also list potters' stamps and furnish a basic typology of the plainer wares, provide models for this particular approach. A good number of recent studies, mainly by Italians, follow the same lines, concentrating on particular workshops or museum collections, though publication of the crucial Arezzo collections is still patchy.

Until recently, however, what was lacking in most of these studies was an interest in the procedures of production and a full appreciation of the geographical spread of sigillata production in Italy at large. Broken moulds, decorative punches and the occasional waster furnish almost all the published evidence from the Arezzo potteries; for other aspects of production (see figs. 5–7 for some possible solutions) we rely on the analogy of finds from Gaul and the German frontier. The identification of other regional Italian fabrics by, for example, chemical analysis has come into its own rather recently, Haltern in Germany (one of the major 'old' sites for the ware) being again a key point of reference. However, the regional production sites remain little studied.[26] The known time-span of the Italian wares has also been expanded by more concentrated work on Mediterranean finds, which include many late types not seen on the northern European sites.

Three regional patterns of production and consumption, rather than one, now seem to emerge. The best known is that seen on the northern and western market (between *c.* 25 BC and AD 25), supplied from Arezzo and its subsidiaries at Pisa and, for a while, Lyon in France. At a later date different sources, in and around the Po Valley, marketed their wares to the north-east, towards the northern Adriatic area and Pannonia; the most common wares here are the relief-decorated cups of Sarius Surus and his associates (col. pl. II *front right*, and fig. 15.2), and vessels with applied motifs. In the third area, comprising the central and eastern Mediterranean coastlands in general, Italian Sigillata wares are not dominant until the reign of Tiberius (AD 14–37), and survived in circulation into the second century; finds of relief wares are rather few, perhaps some 3 per cent of the total. The products of various centres are here mingled: Arezzo products in Augustan times but less so thereafter, the wares of Pozzuoli (Puteoli) and other centres in Campania (perhaps dominant in the period AD 10–50), vessels from Rome itself and elsewhere and, at a late stage, the so-called Late Italian wares which were made mostly in the Pisa region. Concurrently, a thin trickle of South Gaulish Sigillata,[27] mostly of decorated forms like pl. 16 *top*,[28] reached distant Mediterranean markets after *c.* AD 50; their Spanish counterparts are scarcely recorded outside Spain and Morocco.

The new vessel-shapes of Italian Sigillata comprise above all a large series of footed plates with absolutely flat floors, and variously profiled rims. Such plates regularly come in larger and smaller sizes, each with its own treatment of the foot: broad and flat-bottomed on the larger ones (now usually termed 'platters'[29]), and more slender, with a bevelled lower part, on the smaller 'plates' (figs. 13, 14, 16). Bowl-like cups (fig. 17), many with rim and foot treatments matching those of the plates, accompany these. Two major series of

43

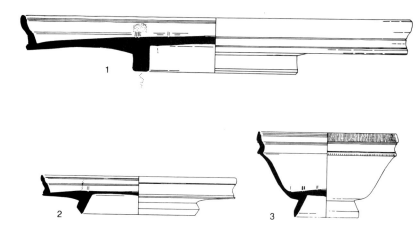

Figure 14 Classic Italian terra sigillata shapes ('Service II') (scale 1:3). (1) Arretine platter (*Conspectus* form 18), stamped CN.ATEI (pl. 5). See also col. pl. II *right*. (2) Arretine plate (*Conspectus* 18), stamped VMBR (pl. 18.3). (3) Cup (*Conspectus* 17), stamped CN ATEI, a variant of the common form 22 (compare fig. 17.4).

matching plates and cups, normally termed 'services' in the specialist literature, typify the Augustan age. In basic terms, one series is early and the other late, though there is a fair overlap. The later one, displaying two rim mouldings separated by a hollow marked off by fine grooves (see fig. 14, and variant pl. 15), was enormously influential on Mediterranean products at large (pl. 14; cf. figs. 3 and 29.1) – it can be considered the Roman shape *par excellence*. Its distinctive features, and those of its successors, were copied (with more or less

Plate 14 Six cups of a typical Roman terra sigillata shape, in various wares (scale *c.* 1:6). *From left, clockwise*: Italian terra sigillata; Eastern Sigillata A ware; Gallo-Belgic *terra rubra*; 'Pontic'. *Centre*: Knidian. *Bottom*: Eastern Sigillata B2 ware.

Plate 15 Arretine cup, bearing rouletting and applied 'spectacle spiral' ornaments (diam. 7.6 cm). Stamp: AVCTVS (see pl. 18.4).

Figure 15 Arretine relief ware (scale 1:3).

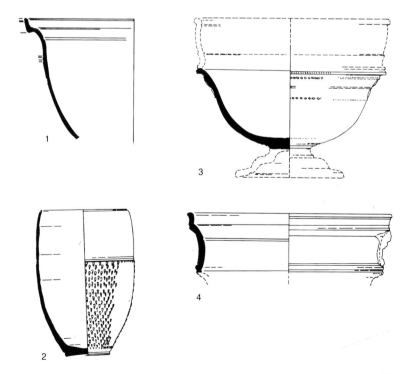

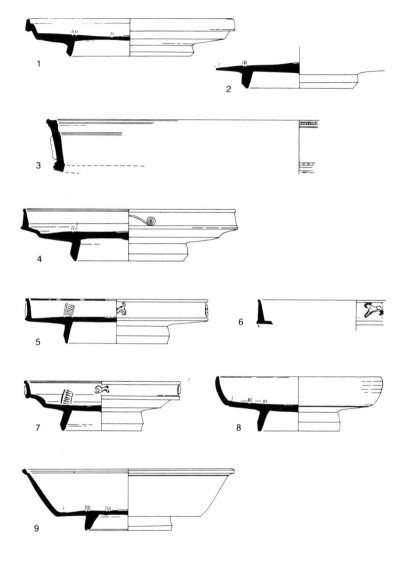

Figure 16 Plate and dish forms (scale 1:3): *Conspectus* forms 2, base as 12 or 18, 20.3 (platter), 21, 20.4 (two), 21 (late), 4 (late), 3.2 respectively. See Index for stamps.

Figure 17 *Opposite page* Cup and bowl forms (scale 1:2):
Conspectus forms 14 (large, small), 15 (large), 22, 32, 26, 27, 33, 36.4, 23.2 (*bottom left*), 34 (*bottom right*) respectively. See Index for stamps.

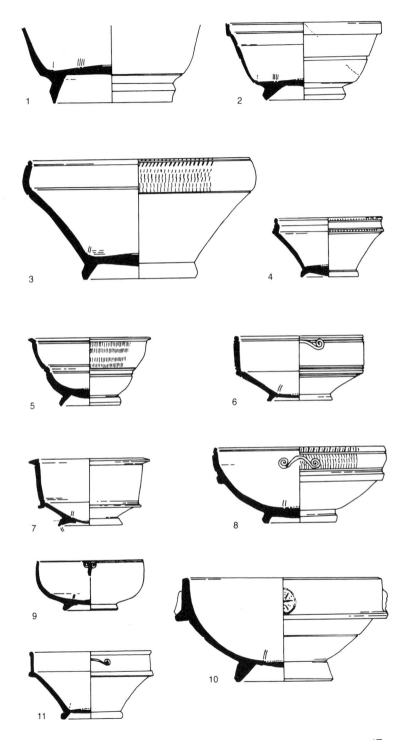

success) by potters as far afield as southern Egypt (see fig. 25.1) and the Crimea (fig. 21 *bottom* and pl. 20 *right* – Italian-style potter's stamp). The earlier series, with elaborate profiling on the inside of the rim (see fig. 17.2), had less influence, since it dates to before the peak in Italian exports. It was more in vogue in the northern Roman provinces.

Among the decorated vessels, the typical shape is a medium-sized bowl set on a pedestal foot (now to be called a 'chalice', in preference to the older term 'crater'). Early examples (see col. pl. II *top centre* and fig. 15.1) have an elegant inverted bell-shaped form, but those from the reign of Tiberius and later (fig. 15.3–4) add a high vertical wall above the decoration, which becomes more stereotyped. A large cylindrical 'beer-mug' shape with a handle at the side (termed a 'modiolus', fig. 5 *right*) is another well-known type. Closed shapes such as jugs are rather rare; the black burial urn (pl. 12) is quite exceptional – it may have been a special commission.

Two centuries of collecting permit many of these regional products, as well as Arezzo finds, to be illustrated from the collections of the British Museum. Attribution of the plain pieces is tentative,

Plate 16 *Top*: South Gaulish relief-decorated bowl by MONTANVS, Dragendorff type 29, a type present on Mediterranean sites, though this bowl was found in London. Diam. 26.0 cm.
Left: signature ('Philo' in Greek) on bottom (exterior) of Gaulish-style bronze bowl (see fig. 2) (scale c. 1:1).

Plate 17 'Late Italian'. *Top*: LR.PIS
(for L. Rasinius Pisanus, a very large
manufacturer), typical coarse rouletting,
Pisa region. 'Found in Köln' - dubious!
Around AD 100. Length of stamp 2.4 cm.
Left: Crescent-shaped (lunate) stamp
SEX.M.P on interior of a decorated bowl
(see pl. 19.5).Width of stamp 2.0 cm.

however, for none have been chemically tested. Some 150 potters'
stamps, representing about a hundred different workshops, are present in the collections (pls. 5, 17, 18, 19.1). Probably less than half of
these are true Arretine since the pattern of acquisitions, mostly from
southern Italy and Rome, has ensured a good mix of other Italian
products. In contrast, the pieces of decorated vessels and of the

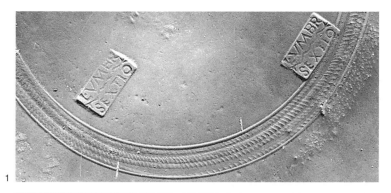

Plate 18 Italian terra sigillata stamps. (1) Early two-line example: L.VMBR[icii] SEXTIO (names of proprietor and slave workman), c. 30–15 BC. Length of stamps 1.7 cm. (2) On relief ware: stamp in relief panel on decorated Arretine-ware chalice (fig. 15.3) by P. Cornelius. The letters RNE form a monogram. Width of stamp 1.55 cm. (3) Normal rectangular shape: VMBR (for Umbricius; cf. (1) above). Length of stamp 1.15 cm. (4) Rectangular variant, indented ends: AVCTVS ('increase' or 'profit' – a typical slave's name), c. 10 BC–AD 25. Length of stamp 1.2 cm. (5) ZOELI (=zoili), in three-lobed stamp. Scale c. 1:1. (6) Foot-shaped (*planta pedis*) form. SEX.M.CL. A typical late stamp, of a proprietor with full three-part Roman citizen's name (as often, abbreviated). Length of stamp 2.3 cm.

Plate 19 Various styles of decoration on Italian relief wares (scale 3:5).
(1, 2) Scenes from mythology (dancing, satyrs, Hercules), classic Arezzo wares.
(3) Masks and garlands, repeated, provincial workshop. (4) Classic Augustan floral scroll, Arezzo. (5) Late debased patterning, Pisa region.

moulds for them are generally Arezzo finds, from old digs in the original kiln-dumps. These show that diverse decorative styles existed side by side (for examples of this see pl. 19). Free-flowing compositions, mainly with scenes from mythology, are outnumbered by decorative arrangements of stock motifs, normally repeated to create a rough symmetry. Some later products show that individual motifs were copied by moulding until they were almost unrecognisable. A very debased Late Italian version is shown in pl. 19.5.

After about AD 75, the main export centre was the region of Pisa, where the so-called Late Italian Sigillata was produced until the mid-second century. A debased mouldmade relief ware was made here, influenced by the technically superior South Gaulish decorated wares of the period, such as pl. 16 *top*. Many of the figure-motifs, which are repeated as appliqués on the walls of the much more numerous plain-ware cups and dishes (pl. 39 *bottom*), derive from earlier Arretine patterns of a couple of generations earlier. A few large proprietors controlled this production, notably one L. Rasin(ius) Pis(anus); their stamps are either foot-shaped (pl. 17 *top*) or of crescent form (pl. 17 *left*), as on contemporary stamped bricks. Individual artisans within these undertakings are no longer named.

Eastern and miscellaneous sigillata wares

The main traditions of sigillata wares in the East, those of Asia Minor and of Syria, are each represented in the British Museum by a fair number of vessels. Both began around 150 BC, much earlier than the Italian wares; early specimens reflect different decorative styles, and are not always red-surfaced. However, starting from around 10 BC–AD 10, they widely imitate the Italian wares. The Asia Minor workshops, some of which were Italian-owned, whole heartedly accepted the new fashions for angular shapes with fine mouldings, and the practice of adding makers' stamps. In Syria and the more distant centres the new influences are somewhat

Plate 20 Stamps on Eastern Sigillata wares and derivatives. *Left*: KAICV ('and you too' - a good luck greeting), Eastern Sigillata A. Length of stamp 1.2 cm. *Right*: *planta pedis* stamp on a local sigillata-style plate, from the Crimea (fig. 21.3 *bottom*).

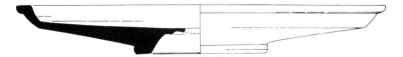

Figure 18 Eastern Sigillata A platter, found in Nubia (scale 1:4).

modified – for instance, potters' stamps appear in a more random fashion, and almost always in Greek (pl. 20 *left*). These eastern wares, whose fabrics can be distinguished by an expert eye, show some peculiar features. For instance, the treatment of feet and bases tends to vary from ware to ware: low feet, often marked off by tiny grooves and ridges, on Eastern Sigillata B, stepped insets on the bottoms of Eastern Sigillata A, and so on (figs. 18–20).

Five widely exported red-gloss wares embody the sigillata tradition in the eastern half of the Roman Empire. Since only one of

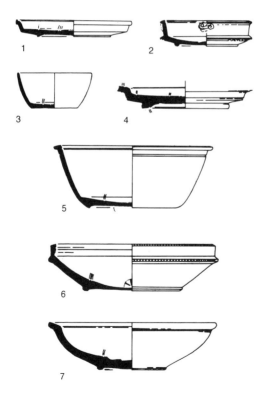

Figure 19 Eastern Sigillata B, various forms (scale 1:3).

these has a clearly documented source – the Pergamon area – they are generally known by the anonymous tags Eastern Sigillata 'A', 'B', 'C', etc. Here I use regional names – even if they are not strictly justified – wherever possible, in order to overcome the different usages of various authors. The true sources of the common Eastern Sigillata A ware (once wrongly named 'Pergamene'), somewhere in the Syrian region, remain elusive – the region of eastern Cilicia north of Iskenderun is now mooted. Those of the 'B' ware, in western Turkey, should include Tralles (mentioned in a text of Pliny the Elder), with Ephesos apparently its main export outlet. The Pergamon regional series was made at Pergamon itself and on the nearby coast at Çandarlı, which has served as a useful tag for the ware at large; along with its forerunners it comprises three or four parallel or overlapping series. Cypriot Sigillata is so named because of its prevalence in Cyprus, though some nearby regions have yielded much of it. Pontic Sigillata here denotes one or more related wares from the shores of the Black Sea, whether made in the Istanbul region, the Crimea or elsewhere. The kiln-sites remain unclear.

These five wares, with their interlocking but distinct patterns of export, share some common traits. There is, for instance, the copying of Italian Sigillata shapes and, less consistently, of their potters' stamps – features mostly confined to the first century AD. Also common, though not on all wares, is the so-called 'double-dipping streak' noted on p. 22 above (see pl. 6). Other features, such as applied motifs on the rim, or barbotine ornaments, here copied from the Italian 'thin-walled' wares, are much rarer. All five wares have their own versions of the plate and matching cup with upright moulded rim (E. Ettlinger *et al.*, *Conspectus* forms 17–19, 22; pl. 14), which are quintessentially Arretine. However, earlier and later vessel-shapes in these wares owe less to the Italian potters; indeed, the later ones are often closer to known metalware types. Some poor copies of Italian relief-decorated bowls are present in Eastern Sigillata A, overlapping the end of a production of relief bowls of Hellenistic shape; better ones are seen rarely at Pergamon (compare the various lead-glazed wares of Asia Minor, for example col. pl. V *right*).

The Asia Minor wares of the early first century AD are the most blatantly 'Italian' in treatment, with their small, neat stamps, sharply articulated mouldings, and penchant (though not at Pergamon) for rouletted ornament (fig. 19). Two of the Eastern Sigillata B(1) workshops seem to be Italian foundations: C. SENT –

Figure 20 *Opposite page*: Eastern Sigillata A, various forms (scale 1:3).

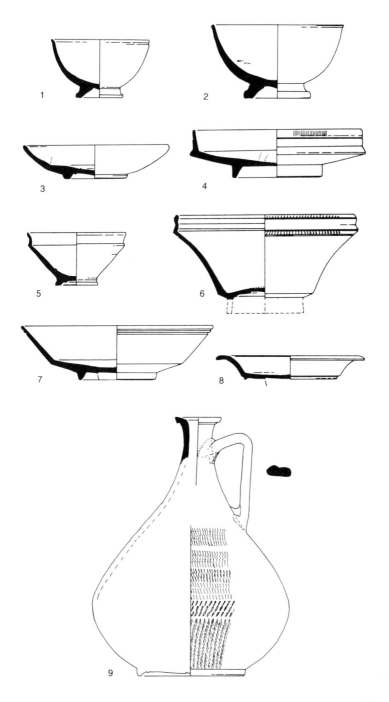

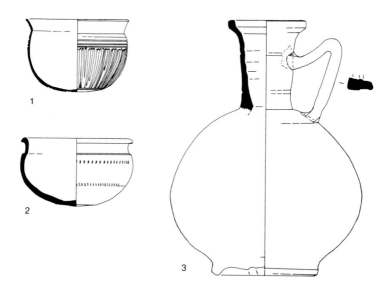

Figure 21 Other Eastern Sigillata wares
(scale 1:3).
Top: Cypriot Sigillata.
Bottom: 'Pontic' terra sigillata and related.

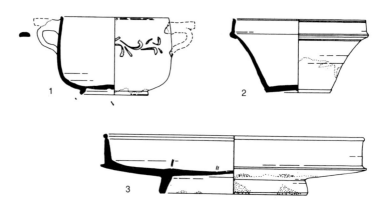

from Arezzo; SERENI – probably from Pozzuoli. A few vessels of this ware bear the (Latin) stamp ARRE/TINA, proclaiming their parentage – though not their actual place of origin! In the fashion current in Asia Minor, Latin and Greek were used interchangeably. The stamps on the other Eastern wares, more variable in form, are almost always in Greek lettering, though the actual names thus recorded (which may include those of slaves and freedman) are sometimes Roman in origin (e.g. *Loukios* for *Lucius*). These eastern potters' stamps are almost all more or less square or rectangular; the foot-shaped (*planta pedis*) type of stamp current on the later Italian wares is at best rare, paralleling a decline in the importation of the Italian models after *c.* AD 30. When the latter picked up again later in the century, the eastern fashion for potters' stamps had all but passed. Foot-shaped stamps, while they occur, are generally uninscribed (though for an early signed one, see pl. 20 *right*).

Eastern Sigillata A ware (figs. 6, 18, 20) illustrates three successive stylistic trends, in part matched on the other wares. Until the time of Christ, its most characteristic shapes are platters with narrow, very thick bases which provide stability to the finished product. These in part mirror metalware, in part late Italian black-gloss ware types. Groups of rouletted circles, often flanking a band with small palmette stamps, decorate their floors. During the first century AD, the flat-floored Italian shapes are in fashion; the bottoms of these commonly feature one or more 'steps'. In a final phase, the shapes tend to copy fashions in metalware, with a series of flat-based dishes and bowls supported on small ledges at the outer edge. Comparable developments occur in the other eastern wares, though only from the time of Augustus onwards. The properties of the various clays, and local traditions, are seen in differing foot-profiles. The high, angular ring-feet of Italian products are copied at Pergamon and on various minor regional wares; those of Eastern Sigillata A ware are simpler (replacing an earlier foot-treatment with a projecting moulding at the base), while on Eastern Sigillata B dishes a low ledge, moulded on the inner face, is substituted (see fig. 19.1; cups may have heavy pedestal-like bases). The late range of Italian Sigillata forms, relatively little copied elsewhere, forms the basis of the late Pergamon (Çandarlı) repertoire. The latter, very similar in both clay and gloss appearance to the Italian wares, are distinguished by extremely thick and heavy bases, and by pronounced scratches on their exteriors (see fig. 3.3). The deep imprints of three clay pads (kiln-separators) often appear on their floors and they generally lack any decoration.

While the Italian wares are the major inspiration during the first century AD, some cross-influences can also be observed. The 'motto'-type stamps on Eastern Sigillata B are repeated on Eastern

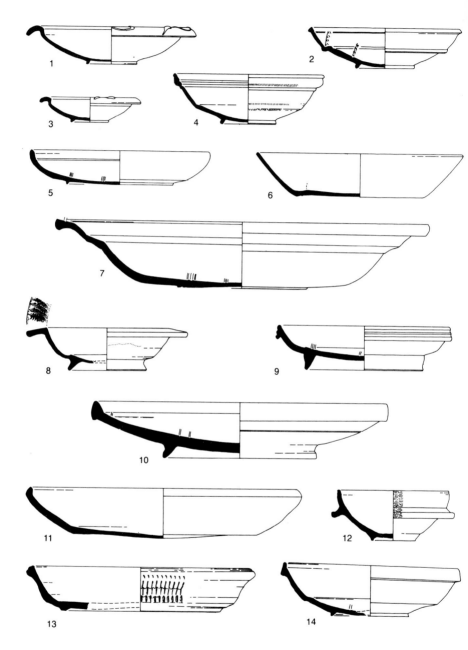

Figure 22 African Red Slip ware and related (scale 1:4). (11) 'Tripolitanian Red Slip' dish. (12) Egyptian (Fayum). (13) Cypriot. (14) Egyptian (Aswan).

58

Sigillata A (pl. 20 *left*), and one bowl-form of the latter has a stepped pedestal base of 'B' type. Several features of Cypriot Sigillata (fig. 21 *top*) seem to copy the 'A' ware – the stepped bottoms of the latter are rendered in the former by gouged-out hollows, often ringed by a deep groove, and the small 'saucers' of the Cypriot ware should derive from a flat-based 'A' ware type. However, a round-bowled 'crater'-form peculiar to Cypriot Sigillata is more likely to be directly modelled on a late Hellenistic metalware shape; its larger versions rest on three moulded 'knucklebone' feet.[30]

African Red Slip ware and other Late Roman fine wares

From the late first century AD onwards, the red-gloss terra sigillata wares were progressively replaced in the Mediterranean Roman market by less sophisticated wares with smooth red-slipped surfaces. North African products, made at first in the Carthage region, and soon followed by the products of related factories in various parts of (modern) Tunisia and eastern Algeria (the ancient provinces of Africa, Byzacena and Numidia), were the leaders in this development. These utilised clays of fairly simple composition (with simple iron compounds, quartz sand and lime impurities, and little else) which did not require such closely controlled firing as those used for sigillata. In addition, the vessel-shapes produced (fig. 22 *top*), like those of the later Eastern Sigillata B ware (fig. 19.3, 5–7), had low feet and were easy to stack for shipping. Hence they could presumably be produced and marketed far more cheaply than the Italian wares. African cooking wares (such as fig. 32.4) led the way, on a small scale, in the first century, and during the second and third centuries the red-slipped tablewares gradually ousted their competitors almost everywhere. For a time in the fourth century they were effectively without rivals, until deliberate imitations of them began to proliferate.

The exported versions of African Red Slip ware comprise three major series – Terra Sigillata africana 'A', 'C' and 'D' in current Italian terminology (the former 'B' series designates the south French series noted below, p. 62). The 'A' ware, somewhat sandy and with a continuous slip coating (generally polished), comprises products from the region of Carthage of the period *c*. AD 75–300, and some close copies. The 'D' wares are their later counterparts, made in a number of centres, mainly in northern Tunisia; on these the slip coating covers only the interior and the rim (or exterior wall). In contrast, the 'C' fabric from central Tunisia is very smooth, with a thin slip coating, mostly absorbed into the surface; the majority of

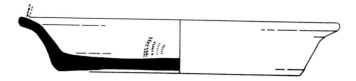

Figure 23 Dish, late Roman, South France, found at Conjux (scale 1:3).

the examples – if not all – appear to have been produced in moulds. This series was made from about AD 220 to 500; a large production of mouldmade lamps parallels the later types.

The shapes of the early African ware comprise smallish dishes and bowls with low feet. Some of these, such as fig. 22.1–3, were modelled on common Italian and South Gaulish Sigillata forms, for instance the wide-rimmed dish – Dragendorff type 36 – which here, as in the Spanish Sigillata wares, retains its typical barbotine leaf patterns. A distinctive version of the carinated bowl (Dragendorff 29), bearing rouletting only, was also created (fig. 22.4). Some mugs and small jugs, often derived from the western 'thin-walled' wares (see below, p. 68; pl. 24, fig. 28.1) accompany them. The later versions of all these became larger, losing their decoration and their polished surfaces. Around AD 200 a new range of broader, flatter dishes came in, some of which were highly polished. The 'C' wares of the third century and later (here fig. 22.6) consciously ape metalware in both thinness and their choice of shapes: large platters, a large dish with straight sloping sides, small bowls with wide, flat rims. Comparable shapes (mostly wide, flat-bottomed dishes) occur in the parallel 'D' ware (pl. 22 *top*, fig. 22.7, and regional variant fig. 22.11), indicating a general shift in the function of these tablewares. The large dish/small bowl contrast lasts until the demise of the

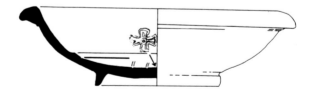

Figure 24 Bowl, Egyptian Red Slip B ware, stamped (scale 1:3).

Figure 25 *Opposite page:* Aswan wares, early to late (scale 1:4).
(1, 2) (Early Roman) copies of faience and sigillata wares.
(3) Painted fish pattern, 4th century.
(4-8) 'Egyptian Red Slip A', late 4th–8th century.
(9) `Costrel' with cream slip, c. AD 350–450 (drawings by P. Roberts).

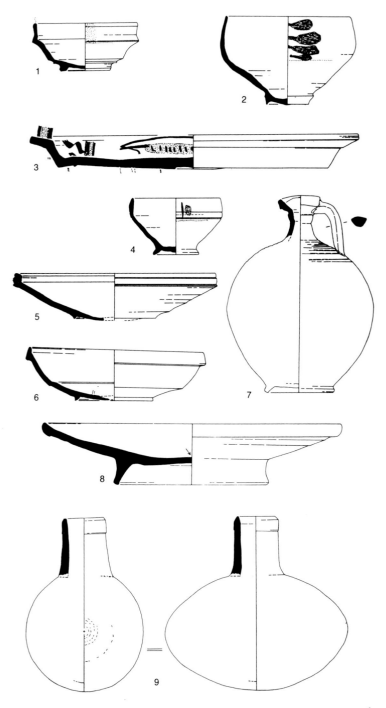

Plate 21 African Red Slip ware fragments with applied or moulded relief ornament, c. AD 360–400+ (scale c. 1:3).

ware in the seventh century. During the fifth century higher foot-rings – some thrown separately and attached – reappear, as they do on metalware (fig. 22.9, 10). Applied ornaments, some arranged to form continuous scenes, appear on the 'C' ware of the third and fourth centuries (pl. 21); a few relief-decorated vessels could even be cast-off metal originals. Stamped patterns, at first floral but increasingly figurative (pl. 22), were introduced on both wares around AD 325 and lasted until the later sixth century. Crosses and other Christian motifs adorn fifth- and sixth-century products. Almost all these features and trends are matched on metalware of the period.

As noted above, fine-ware imitations of these wares appear from the fourth century onwards. Some of the closest copies are found in Egypt, an area which had remained outside the mainstream of Roman pottery fashions until this period. The large potteries of the Aswan area produced and exported African-style stamped wares in quantity; fifth-century African shapes persisted here until the eighth century and later (fig. 25.5–6, 8). Some of these bear painted texts (pl. 2). Other, less delicate versions of these types were made elsewhere in Egypt (figs. 22.12 and 24) and Cyprus (fig. 22.13). At the other end of the Mediterranean, African and Phocean (see below) shapes were grafted on to the pre-existing Hispanic sigillata tradition, which enjoyed a final flourish in the late fourth and fifth centuries. A South Gaulish counterpart of simpler manufacture is illustrated in fig. 23.

More independent of the African wares, and in terms of fabric and technique a continuation of the Pergamon/Çandarlı terra sigillata tradition, is the Phocean Red Slip ware from the west coast of Turkey (Asia Minor), dating from c. 350–550 and continuing on a reduced scale until after AD 650. Its initial fortunes seem to be linked to the fourth-century growth of the eastern Roman capital of Constantinople, which it was well placed to service; thereafter, it served much of the eastern and central Mediterranean. This ware, of which complete preserved examples are few – they do not occur in

Plate 22 African Red Slip ware: stamped ornament. *Top*: bowl from Carthage region. Found in Egypt, *c.* AD 400. Diam. 41.0 cm. *Bottom left*: detail of dish, *c.* AD 400 (scale *c.* 2:5). *Bottom right*: plate fragment with *chi-rho* motif, *c.* AD 460–500 (scale 2:3).

Byzantine Christian burials – may have been part-fabricated in moulds; notable features are a marked thinning out of the sides towards the mid-point, and 'scratched' outer surfaces. Their rims are often discoloured (black, for instance) on the outside, the only part of the vessel exposed during firing, since this was done in stacks.

Early examples of this ware imitate the shapes and floral stamps of the African wares, but after about AD 420 these develop differently. The classic vessel-shape is a deep dish or shallow bowl with an upright projecting rim, which in the course of a century develops a more and more pronounced overhang (see fig. 3.2, 3 for the developed shape). The broad bands of rouletting often seen on the rims and floors of these dishes are impressed with an implement with three or more rows of teeth – a technique copied on some other Asia Minor wares of the period. The stamps, mostly a simple impressed outline, have a 'childish' quality.

The Cypriot Sigillata series noted above revived in the later sixth and seventh centuries, producing a series of distinctive flat-based dishes, some bearing a simple stamped cross at the centre.

The varying fortunes of these later Roman stamped wares are perhaps best seen on the Palestinian and Nile Delta sites, where no local good-quality tablewares were available as competitors. The Phocean ware, and some African products, are on occasion found as far afield as western Britain (see sherds in fig. 3).

Derivatives of these wares, generally with painted decoration (e.g. col. pl. VII), continued to be made in Egypt, and especially in Nubia, well into the Islamic period. Another painted red-slipped ware of high quality comes from the Jerash region of Jordan during the sixth and seventh centuries; it derives from a small regional class of close imitations of the stamped African wares.

LEAD- AND ALKALINE-GLAZED WARES

Lead-glazed pottery appears intermittently throughout the Roman Empire from the later first century BC onwards. In the Mediterranean world it was never common, though some large-scale production, not relevant here, occurred in Pannonia and in the far north of Italy in the fourth and earlier fifth centuries. Only in the seventh and eighth centuries, in Constantinople, did lead-glazed tablewares begin to come into regular use.

The earliest such wares can be seen as one of a number of alternatives to luxury silver and gold plate, whose forms and ornamentation they mimic. Like glassware, and the glass-frit vessels noted below, they offer a new range of colours – green, yellow and brown

Plate 23 Lead-glazed drinking-vessel, found at Tharros, Sardinia (tomb 33), late 1st century AD (scale 1:3).

Figure 26 Lead-glazed jar, 'Rome' series, 2nd century AD (scale 1:3).

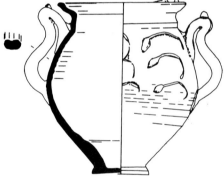

– for standard types of vessels. Most appear to have been fired in stacks within closed containers known as saggars; scars left by the stilts which separated the vessels during firing may be visible on the floors and elsewhere. Remains of such stacking equipment, along with various waste materials, are known from a workshop site at Perge in Pamphylia (southern Turkey). The glaze employed was generally fairly thick, tending to crack and to run. Accumulations of glaze at the rim or base indicate which way up the vessel was stacked for firing. Certain Asia Minor products, however, from Mytilene (see col. pl. V *right*), and perhaps from the Pergamon region, display a thinner, even glaze and lack the stacking scars; it is not clear how their glaze material was applied. Common to both

65

series is the priming of the hollows in the moulds with white clay before the vessels were formed, to create highlighted motifs on the finished, glazed, pots (col. pl. V); white barbotine motifs, added just before the glazing, were an alternative.

The early drinking vessels carried mouldmade relief decoration, comparable in style and motifs to Italian Sigillata, and are represented in the British Museum's collections by specimens from various places. Most were probably made in western Asia Minor; the wares of the two important export centres at Perge and Mytilene, mentioned above, are almost certainly represented (col. pl. V *right*), along with others less well documented. In other regions we know of a workshop located by excavation at Tarsus in the east, while centres in Italy and possibly south Gaul – mostly unlocated – also made the standard types: a shallow cup ('scyphus') with spurred handles, a deeper version of the same ('cantharus') and a chalice comparable to Arretine ware products (col. pl. II *top centre*). These generally date from the first century AD – some of the latest dated examples are furnished by Pompeii. A thin-walled class with small, applied, decorative plaques appears to stem from southern Italy (col. pl. V *left*) although the production centre is not known; from the same source come small 'askos' jugs with relief vine or ivy motifs. Barbotine ornament is used elsewhere; spine-like motifs and leaf patterns are seen on a rather later (second- to early third-century) ware from the region of Rome (fig. 26). A plain glazed vessel from the same source is shown at pl. 23. Late Roman specimens from Mediterranean countries are rare, though offshoots of the north Italian products of this period are noted from Rome.

Mention must be made of a category of glazed vessels made in glass frit (commonly but erroneously termed 'faience') current in Egypt. This self-glazing material had been used there for millennia to produce small moulded ornaments and figurines, but in Hellenistic and early Roman times was put to use for vessels of some size. The Roman series of the first to second centuries AD has a brighter, more glassy glaze than before, resulting from the addition of lead oxide to the glaze mix (copying lead-glazed pottery). The angular shapes of plain terra sigillata (fig. 14) are imitated here, in a heavier, thicker form.[31]

A similar alkaline glaze mix was favoured on the buff-ware pottery of Mesopotamia in the Parthian period (roughly from the first century BC to the third century AD). Though present on Roman sites on the eastern frontier, such wares hardly ever reached the Mediterranean. Their shapes are more Hellenistic than Roman; early versions dating to the Seleucid period occur at Antioch.

THIN-WALLED WARES

The plates and bowls in terra sigillata were complemented, for table use, by a class of drinking vessels in a very thin and light-weight fabric, generally going under the name of 'thin-walled' wares (for examples, see fig. 27 and pl. 24). Many of these can be seen as conscious copies of vessels in other materials, in particular silver plate and, at a later stage, glassware. Originating probably in northern Italy in the second century AD, they are typical of the new wave of Italian 'Roman' tablewares of the period 100 BC to AD 100. The locations of several of the workshops/factories are known either from literary sources or through excavation. These Italian products were imitated, especially during the first century AD, by a number of provincial workshops, in north-western Asia Minor, southern and central Gaul, Spain (particularly Baetica in the south) and the Alpine regions, extending to the Danube.[32]

While some of these are wheel-thrown in the normal way, others

Plate 24 Thin-walled wares. *Top*: late 1st-century BC types from Grave 53 (initial burial), Tharros, Sardinia (scale 1:5). *Bottom*: Two-handled cup (derived from 'thin-walled' shape) and bowl (modelled on Gaulish Sigillata) in slip-coated ware (red slip, rouletted decoration). Southern France, 2nd century AD and later (scale 1:4).

(and perhaps not just those bearing relief patterns) were made in moulds, like the decorated sigillata wares which they can resemble in fabric. Attempts to emulate the thinness of metalware and glass led to the production in quite large numbers of very delicate and fragile bowls and beakers. These were around a millimetre in thickness (fig. 27.2, for instance) and it is difficult to imagine them being made freehand on a potter's wheel in the numbers evidently demanded. The delicately formed handles, however, were generally added freehand, as was the ornament, which was varied: rouletting (fig. 27.2) and barbotine (fig. 27.10) were the commonest. Barbotine and 'rough-cast' decoration (the scattering or brushing of fine grits on to the pot, to produce a rough surface) are particularly typical of these wares. Some variants, such as roller-stamping, are also illustrated here. Like the vessels in more precious materials that they copy, some (mainly the earlier types) have a plain body, with the ornament restricted to the handles, which can be elaborately treated, sometimes with decorative thumb-rests and spurs (fig. 27.1; cf. col. pl. V *right*). The bases are usually flat and without projecting feet, thus avoiding problems if encasing moulds were used. Many vessels were evidently fired in vertical stacks, leaving most of the outer surfaces to be exposed to changing conditions in the kiln, which turned them grey. This two-colour effect (grey and yellow/brown) was sometimes exploited to provide a contrast with added ornament on the wall, as on the Egyptian (Nubian) specimens, (col. pl. IV and fig. 28 *bottom*).

The typical shapes are beakers and small drinking bowls without handles, as well as versions of these – cups – provided with two handles (fig. 27). These latter could be cupped in the hand of a person taking a meal or drinking while reclining on a couch according to approved Mediterranean custom; the handles may have served for setting the cup down on a side-table as much as for actual use for drinking. The ornamented body-surface would provide a firm grip for the user. Mugs with handles, more suited to users who were seated or standing, are typical of one or two series only; their handles are generally attached to the body (fig. 28.1). In Gallic and northern lands, the shallow cups give way to mugs and larger beakers which copy the decorative treatments of the Mediterranean wares while pointing to different habits of use.

After c. AD 60–80, the Italian products were succeeded by two series of thin-walled mugs from the eastern Aegean, with handles set close to the rim, and two-colour firing after the Italian manner. One, with a high offset rim (see pl. 25 *left*), was produced at Phocea in Asia Minor, while the other (fig. 28.2 and pl. 25 *right*), with a low rim marked off by a small external ridge (*collarino*, in Italian parlance) comes from some unlocated centre on the coast of Thrace or

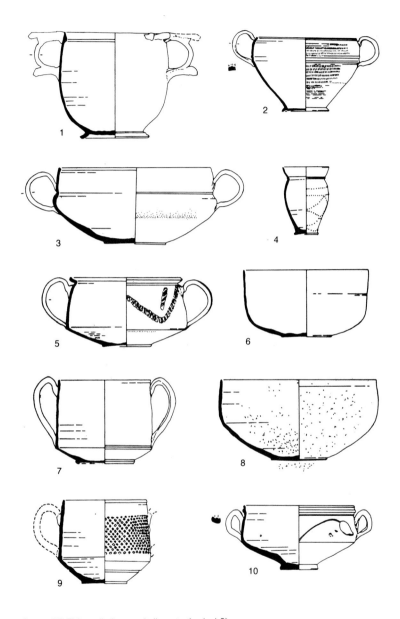

Figure 27 Thin-walled wares, Italian, etc. (scale 1:3).

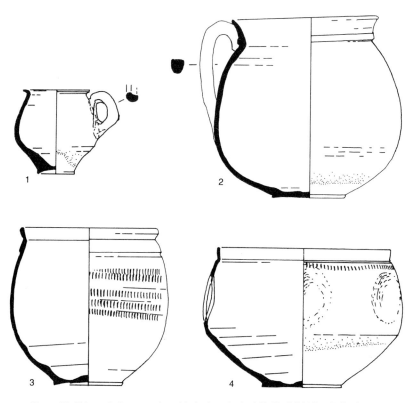

Figure 28 Thin-walled ware variants/derivatives (scale 1:2). (3, 4) Nubian derivatives.

around the Dardanelles. This appears sometimes to have been given a salt-water wash before firing; when overfired it occasionally appears salt-glazed. During the second and early third centuries both series were exported *en masse* to the south and west, as far as the northern Adriatic and Rome, in company with the Phocean cooking wares. Some late examples of the second type bear white painted ornaments or motto-like inscriptions in Greek (pl. 25 *right*); the type and the tags are copied on slip-coated mugs made in Athens after *c*. AD 200.[33]

A separate, earlier tradition of thin-walled vessels, deriving from Hellenistic black-gloss wares, is seen at Knidos in Asia Minor ('Knidian Grey Ware'). The typical shape here is an angular ('carinated') bowl with thin handles, twisted upwards to form cross-bars flanking the rim (fig. 29.2). Such bowls, in some cases stamped on the inside in the Hellenistic manner, were exported a good deal in Augustan times, and survived until about AD 100.

Plate 25 Thin-walled mugs, late 1st to early 3rd century AD. *Left*:'Aegean' (Phocaea) type. *Right*:Thracian (?) 'a collarino' type, late version with white painted inscription in Greek:'Eutuchia' ('Good Fortune'). Height 12.6 cm, 8.9 cm.

Figure 29 Knidian, grey and coarse wares (scale 1:3).

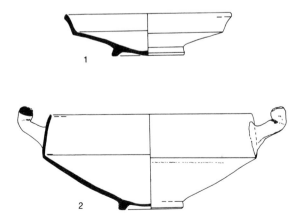

Other 'fine' wares

Two distinctive series of containers, found thinly scattered all over the Mediterranean (and on occasions further afield), may have owed their popularity to their contents, perhaps prized as medicine or even aphrodisiacs. The mouldmade Knidian relief ware (pl. 26) comes in a variety of closed shapes, ranging from ornamental jugs to vessels in the form of anatomical parts (especially phallus-shaped

Plate 26 *Top:* Mouldmade table-amphora (*oinophoros*), Knidian relief ware, front and back. Dionysiac scenes (satyrs and maenads), 2nd century AD. Height 24.3 cm.
Left: hollow handles of shallow bowls (*paterae*) for ritual use. Mouldmade, with animal-head terminals, Knidian fabric, 2nd century AD (scale c. 1:2).

Plate 27 *Top*: Corinthian relief-ware bowl, battle with Amazons, 3rd century AD. Diam. 11.9 cm. *Right*: small mouldmade double flask, Harpokrates and swags. Egyptian, probably Memphis ware, early Roman? (scale 3:5).

vases).[34] Alongside these are versions of the jugs and bowls with tubular animal-headed handles (normally metalware forms) commonly used for religious rituals. In contrast to the sigillata wares, these are orange or brown, with a slip of similar colour, perhaps meant to recall bronze. They span the period *c.* AD 70–250. Corinthian relief ware, typically in the form of small vertical-sided bowls with mould-formed relief friezes (fig. 30 and pl. 27 *top*), spans the third century; no lids are known, but some means of closing them is likely. The Dionysiac and other scenes on them, mostly very

Figure 30 Corinthian relief bowl (see pl. 27 *top*) (scale 1:3).

poorly modelled, hardly relate closely to their presumed contents. Some of the Knidian types are revived in North Africa (in red-slip wares) around AD 300.

Some other vessels in the form of figurines are known, mostly in early Roman times. A few from south Russian sites seem derived from Hellenistic forebears. In Egypt the tradition of small mould-made figured vases and figurines functioning as lamps continued more vigorously than elsewhere. A double unguent-vase with figures (pl. 27 *right*) here illustrates a class of small vessels made around 100 BC–AD 100 in the Memphis and Bubastis areas. Two examples of head-shaped form, in a hard-fired red ware with a 'metallic' slip, from an unidentified source in the western or central part of the Nile Delta (col. pl. VI), may be influenced by the Knidian wares; they are matched by a class of second-century clay lamps.

COARSE WARES

BUFF WARES: CLOSED FORMS

In Roman times, following earlier Greek fashion, clays firing to a cream or buff tint were used widely for jugs, flagons and other serving vessels. The surface of these was generally left unsealed, allowing a certain amount of evaporation; when the contents had to be retained (as in amphorae for shipment) a deliberate coating of

Plate 28 Lagynos-type flagons.
Left: probably Tripolitanian, polished surface (scale *c.* 1:4). *Bottom left*: Sardinian, red, polished. Height 17.0 cm.
Bottom right: probably Cypriot, red slip. Height 13.1 cm.

Plate 29 Plain kitchen-ware jug, ribbed. Found at Carthage, 4th–5th century AD (scale c. 1:3).

resin or the like was applied to the inner surface. Some finer versions, for table use, were coated with a slip of similar colour. Recurrent shapes include narrow-necked flagons, derived from the Hellenistic *lagynos* type and mostly with a globular or ovoid body (pl. 28),[35] which were popular in the first centuries BC and AD. Similar shapes are seen in the sigillata wares.

Ribbed bodies, handles of the 'sliced' variety, and indented bases with central 'buttons' are recurrent features of the later varieties, in common with the cooking wares of the period (see fig. 4 and pl. 7; also the late Carthage example, pl. 29).

Heavy-duty kitchen wares, principally basins and rough lids, were also regularly made in uncoated buff wares.

COOKING WARES

The basic cooking-ware shapes used in Mediterranean lands in Roman times were round-bottomed cooking pots and casseroles (pl. 30 and fig. 31), usually with small handles set close to the rim, often with provision for a lid, which was normally of shallow conical shape with a small central knob. These were made in both oxidised

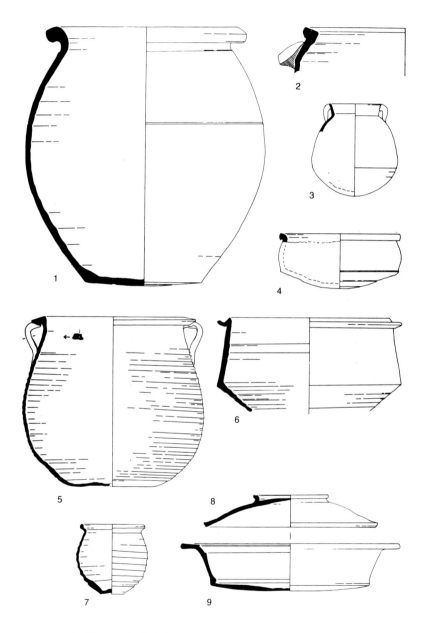

Figure 31 Cooking pots (scale: 1:4).

Plate 30 Cooking pots, Egyptian, 1st–3rd century AD (scale 1:4).

(red, brown) and reduced (grey) fabrics. Like the Greek and Hellenistic types from which they derive, these are generally rather thin-walled, allowing rapid transmission of heat, and are made of refractive (heat-resistant) fabrics, containing an admixture of sand or similar material. In this they contrast with the wares in the Celtic tradition which were made in the northern Roman provinces.

To the basic 'Greek' types were added, from about the second century BC, flat-bottomed pans suitable for baking (fig. 32). The best known of these bear a smooth 'non-stick' red coating on the interior, and go by the name of 'Pompeian Red ware'. (The name describes the colour of the slip, matching the common red tint of wall plaster at Pompeii; the fact that one series actually comes from the same region is fortuitous.) Such vessels, made in the Naples/Pompeii area and elsewhere in south-central Italy, were widely exported after *c.* 100 BC. In Augustan times they reached both southern England and Petra in Jordan (cf. the Palestinian find, fig. 32.1). Some matching lids are known. Along with these travelled deeper pans with an upright rim bearing a groove on the upper edge (named the 'orlo bifido' type; see fig. 32.3) and shallow lids used as baking covers. The clay body of these contains dark volcanic grits, indicating sources on the west coast of Italy (Campania, etc.). Some later African products derive from these types (e.g. fig. 32.4).

Rival centres in the East include Phocea on the west coast of Turkey, where 'frying pans' with distinctive tubular handles rising

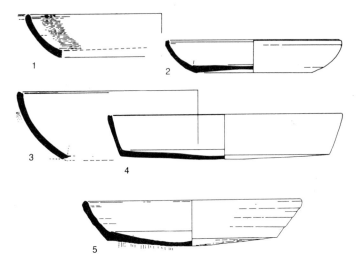

Figure 32 Cooking dishes, Italian and derivatives (scale 1:4).

from the side were produced from the first century BC onwards. Its other products include mugs in thin fabric (see above), flat-rimmed cooking dishes with a red wash modelled on the 'Pompeian Red' imports, and a large series of finely ribbed cooking wares (deep pots, casseroles, jugs: see fig. 31.5–7). The latter (e.g. fig. 31.5) have small handles of the 'sliced' variety noted above (p. 24). Such vessels are common in the period c. AD 60–250 on sites around the Aegean

Figure 33 Cooking pots, Levant (scale 1:3).

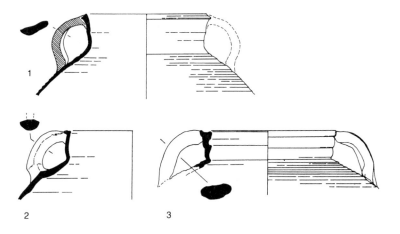

and up the Adriatic, where they generally supplanted the earlier Italian exports.

Rather shallower versions of the round-bodied cooking pot are current in the Levant (including Cyprus) throughout Roman times (fig. 33). These, often of extreme thinness, share the ribbed treatment and 'sliced' handles. Casseroles with closely fitted lids (actually made as a single vessel and then sliced apart) are also common here. These seem to reflect Jewish culinary needs, in terms of ritual purity, but may later have been adopted by Christians and others. The type appears by AD 100 and is current for some six centuries. Another type of casserole, flat-rimmed, has a flat 'saucepan' handle folded back in 'wishbone' shape.

MORTARIA

Buff- and cream-ware *mortaria* (bowls for grinding and preparing food, for kitchen use), often bearing impressed makers' stamps, were made in Italy and some western centres in the first century AD, continuing a long tradition of the use of such vessels in the Greek world. However, the type soon disappeared from most Mediterranean kitchens, being replaced by similar vessels in stone and marble. In the northern parts of the Empire, though, vessels based on the early Imperial Italian model remained in use throughout Roman times. The basic Italian type (first to second century: fig. 34.2) is larger and heavier than most of the imitations, perhaps indicating the use of rough moulds to accommodate its unwieldy projecting features (now an integral part of the vessel, and not added, as formerly). Most examples bear stamps (e.g. pl. 32 *bottom left*) similar to those found on Roman bricks and tiles, suggesting manufacture in the same workshops, with some techniques shared. A revival of the type, retaining the same shape but with stamps in Greek (fig. 34.3, pl. 32 *bottom right*: detail) is seen in northern Syria in the later third and fourth centuries. The latter class, made in a distinctive dark brown ware containing black volcanic grits, had some success on markets in the Levant, surviving in modified forms into the seventh century. In North Africa a flanged version is found in late Roman times; here pieces of imported lava millstones were sometimes recycled to form the grits. Small non-functional versions of the type occur (pl. 31) after AD 400. Cooking pots, along with their lids, were occasionally (re)used in Roman times to serve as the urns for cremation burials.[36] Sometimes, in Italy, special versions were made for this specific purpose, the name of the deceased being scratched or painted on them (see fig. 31.2 and pl. 32 *top*, an urn from Puteoli (Pozzuoli)).

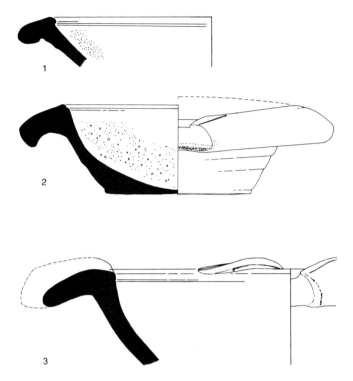

Figure 34 Mortaria (scale 1:4). (1, 2) Italian and related. (1) Stamped SATVRNINI, c. AD 1–60. (2) No stamp, c. 2nd century AD. (3) Syrian, stamped 'Hermogenous', in Greek, c. AD 250–350. Found at Knidos, in the 'Gymnasium' (Newton's excavations, 1859).

Plate 31 Small flanged bowl with gritted interior as on mortaria. The grits may here be mere decoration. North African, found at or near Carthage. 5th or early 6th century AD. Diam. 19.5 cm.

Plate 32 *Top*: cooking vessel used as a cremation urn, with scratched name 'SICABIA CHRESTE'. From the W. Temple Collection, found at Puteoli (modern Pozzuoli), 1st–2nd century AD? Height 22.8 cm, diam. (rim) 22.2–22.6 cm.
Bottom: stamped fragments of mortaria (scale 1:3).
Left: Italian (see fig. 34.1), stamped SATVRNINI.
Right: North Syrian (see fig. 34.3), stamped (in Greek) by Hermogenes, 3rd–4th century AD.

Local Egyptian Wares

Until the fourth century AD, Egypt, home to some 10 per cent of the population (i.e., pottery-users) of the Roman Empire, was something of a world apart, with its own local currency system which tended to keep imports out of the hands of the average peasant. Except in 'foreign' enclaves such as Alexandria, regional self-sufficiency was prevalent. In pottery terms this is seen in a multiplicity of 'local' wares, as yet hardly studied in depth, and in one or two dominant 'regional' wares such as that of Aswan, which was shipped down the Nile in quantity. Most of these wares are based on Nile silt, which fires to a distinctive deep brown and regularly contains gold mica specks. The more mixed clays of the Fayum depression can be reddish, and in the eastern Nile Delta a deep pinkish-red tint is present (see the figure-vase, col. pl. VI). Outside the Nile floodplain sandy buff fabrics are found, and in some places mined clays of glacial origin produce smooth whitish wares (seen both in Nubia – col. pl. IV – and in the Luxor area). The Nile silt is frequently tempered with straw or lime to produce a more durable ware, but some fine-textured wares were also made of it, especially in the Delta region (e.g. the figure-vase, pl. 27 *right*).

Painted decoration often appears on these Egyptian wares, as it had earlier. It was generally applied over a reddish or whitish slip, masking the coarseness of the clay body. An 'early' Roman style emphasises silhouette florals arranged in scrolls, sometimes alternating with bands of cross-hatching (col. pl. III). Old discoveries from Nubia suggest a date around the second century for this, which seems matched stylistically on a series of thin-walled vessels in pale brown (Upper Egyptian?) ware (col. pl. IV, see comments above, p. 68). Considerably later, and found from Upper Egypt down to the Delta, is a class of quite heavy jars bearing bichrome painting in thick black and orange-red paint, often depicting animal and human subjects in a rather crude, lively style. Where datable, these seem to belong to the fifth and sixth centuries. Related painted wares, with somewhat schematic and abstract treatments, appear in Upper Egypt and Nubia at about this time. Some of these, influenced by foreign styles, exhibit a yellow-cream variant of the Aswan fabric. An example of this is a curious type of 'serving dish' (col. pl. VII) with inset circular bowls, matching a rare African Red Slip type of the sixth to seventh centuries. Vessels such as these gave rise in turn to a long tradition of Nubian Christian painted wares, which are beyond the scope of this volume.

The generally rough nature of Egyptian wares is illustrated by the typical amphora shapes, which are heavy, roughly ribbed, and provided with small straw-tempered handles of very crude manufacture (pl. 9 *right*) and poorly attached. A common feature of the smaller flagons for domestic use is a strainer inserted in the base of the neck – presumably to exclude flies and so on. This could be termed an Egyptian peculiarity, and gives a foretaste of the very elaborately patterned strainers developed in medieval Islamic times. Cooking pots bear some resemblance to contemporary Palestinian types (fig. 33.3 and pl. 30 *top*). Favourable soil conditions have often preserved for us the ropes which were attached to the handles of these Egyptian household wares (pl. 35); some other finds are cocooned in protective wrappings (pl. 34 *bottom*). Quite large numbers of complete vessels are preserved in Egypt in domestic rather than funerary contexts, as a result of being sealed under collapsed mud-brick walls and the like. In fact, in Egypt proper (as against Nubia) recorded pots of Roman date from burial contexts are few – many may simply have been removed in antiquity for reuse.

VESSELS WITH
SPECIAL FUNCTIONS

UNGUENTARIA

Small narrow-necked flasks to contain perfumed oils or unguents, (hence the usual name *unguentaria*) were common in the first century AD. They were frequently deposited in burials, presumably to create sweet smells. Their contents are rarely found, since the stoppers were of organic materials which have perished. The usual version of the first century AD has an egg-shaped body with tubular neck; an earlier variety with a spindly toe was common in the Hellenistic world (late Italian versions are seen until about AD 15).

Plate 33 Tomb-group from Byblos (Phoenicia). Clay and glass unguentaria (local) and a clay lamp of Italian shape, c. AD 30–60 (scale c. 2:5).

Plate 34 Unguentaria. *Top centre and right*: standard (Italian) types. *Bottom left*: wrapped Egyptian version. *Top left*: late Asia Minor variant. Height 20.8 cm. Mostly 1st century AD; the two small ones at lower right should date from the time of Augustus.

Classic 'Roman' versions of both of these shapes, in a smooth tan-brown ware with a rather glossy black or brown slip, were made in Italy, perhaps specifically for the perfume industry of Capua. These enjoyed a certain vogue in the provinces (from Britain to Phoenicia and Egypt), presumably as representatives of a Roman life-style, and were much imitated (see pl. 33, from Byblos). By AD 100 they had been largely ousted by versions in glass, though in some provinces, such as Cyprus, clay copies of successive glassware shapes persist. Typical specimens are shown in pl. 34, including one with its ancient wrapping. A luxury silver version is also present in the collections of the British Museum.[37]

RITUAL VESSELS AND RELIGIOUS SOUVENIRS

Small vessels for domestic ritual use are common pottery finds in Italy and the West, at least from the first and second centuries. The most popular type is the so-called *tazza*, a footed bowl with frilled clay bands applied to the exterior, probably used for the burning of incense. The type has also been noted on some eastern sites, such as

Plate 35 Incense burner (with rope attachment). Romano-Egyptian, found at Hawara. Height 18.5 cm.

Plate 36 Christian *ampullae* (small flasks for sanctified oil or water). *Right*: from the St Menas shrine near Alexandria. Motif shows St Menas, with camels at his feet. Diam. *c.* 10.5 cm. *Below left*: Ephesos region, Turkey. Cross. Diam. 2.9 cm. *Below right*: southern Turkey, source unknown. Nativity scenes. Diam. 15.0 cm.

Athens). Square trays with horned sides, set on pedestals, fulfilled a similar function in Egyptian homes (see pl. 35). Votive pots in the Greek tradition are generally scarce, though the jugs and saucepan-like vessels associated with Roman cults are occasionally copied in the East (e.g. pl. 26 *bottom*, Knidian). Vessels made locally for specific cults, bearing applied snakes and other symbols, are sometimes found in Mediterranean contexts.

In later, Christian times small clay vessels were produced in or near several holy places to serve as portable containers for sanctified liquids. Most of these take the form of 'pilgrim-flasks' – vessels with a small spout and handles attached to a flat-sided body, made in moulds, bearing suitable patterns in relief. Such flasks, dating between *c*. AD 400 and 650, come mostly from the eastern Mediterranean (for examples see pl. 36). A number bear Christian inscriptions; best known are those offering a blessing from a local Egyptian saint, Menas, whose shrine lay not far distant from Alexandria.

TOYS

Positive identification of toys is difficult, but some small and miniature vessels found in children's graves may be classed here, rather than as miniature cult vessels (see above). The most distinctive are thin-walled vessels in the form of animals – pigs, for instance – bearing applied glass 'jewels' (pl. 37 *left*); they date from the second century and come from the neighbourhood of Rome.

VARIOUS PRODUCTS

Some plain buff-ware 'tubs' with partially closed mouths, found in Crete, Asia Minor and elsewhere, may have served as portable toilets; others, common on Aegean sites, bearing combed scratches on their inner surfaces and fitted with disc lids, are identified as ceramic beehives. A kind of cylindrical jar in which dormice (a culinary delicacy) were raised has also been identified.

APPENDIX

A BRIEF HISTORY OF THE
BRITISH MUSEUM'S COLLECTION

The British Museum's collections of Roman pottery have long been known to scholars through Walters' classic *Catalogue* of 1908. More recently, C. Johns' brief guide (*Arretine and Samian Pottery*, London 1971) has served as a more popular introduction to the subject. Both were mainly focused on the wares which can be found in Roman Britain, whether made there or (in the case of the well-known red samian ware) in France (Gaul). However, the origins of the latter ware in Italy (at Arezzo and elsewhere) are duly acknowledged in both works.

Plate 37 Early accessions: Sloane Collection (the original 1756 gift). *Left*: small pig vase with glass inlays. Italian (Rome?), 2nd century AD. Length 10.5 cm, height 6.0 cm. *Right*: garum amphora, Spanish type (Dressel 12; Beltrán III/IV; Mau-Schone XIV), 1st century AD.

The 240-odd years of the Museum's existence, from its origins in the Sloane Collection (pl. 37),[38] have spanned the period of the Grand Tour collectors, before the age of modern antiquities laws (pl. 38), as well as that of the peak of the British Empire, when many an administrator or military man amassed his private collection of mementoes (pl. 39 top). In due course many of these collections passed to the British Museum. Others (mostly the prizes of Empire) came to stock many of our provincial museums.[39] Meanwhile the Museum, along with others, was adding to its collections by sponsoring its own excavations abroad, or (when circumstances permitted) by purchase on the open market. It has not always had the pick of what was available – for instance, personal rivalries led to the bulk of Sir Flinders Petrie's finds from Egypt going to University College, London, rather than to the British Museum.

The main Mediterranean sources of Roman pottery in the Museum are – from the early years of the collections – Italy, along with some items from Greece and elsewhere (e.g. pl. 38 top and bottom right), then – from the 1830s onwards – Egypt, joined in colonial times by Cyprus (e.g. pl. 39 top and fig. 21 top) and a small amount from Palestine (figs. 32.1, 3 and 33.1) and Malta (fig. 28.1). Excavations at Tharros in Sardinia (pl. 23, 24 top), at Knidos and Ephesos (figs. 3.2–3, 29.1 and 34.3) in western Turkey, at various locations in Egypt and Nubia (e.g. col. pls. I, III–IV, VI–VII, pl. 9 right and fig. 25), and elsewhere have added their tally – normally, in colonial times, on the basis of a share-out between the host country and the excavators. In recent years the volume of acquisitions has slackened, but host countries have often generously presented sample finds, occasionally of some significance, to the Museum's excavators. New, well-documented material has arrived, for instance, from Sabratha and Benghazi in Libya (pl. 40 and fig. 31.5–6), Petra in Jordan and Hermopolis in Egypt. The occasional diplomatic gift has also accrued to the collections.[40] As a result of this, and of the ancient trading in such wares, the Museum's collections illustrate nearly all the major wares of the period.[41] Most of the items on display are complete vessels, but a considerable collection of fragments (sherds) is also held by the relevant Departments.

Among older acquisitions from private sources, some dubious find-spots are recorded, presumably invented by dealers to attract collectors. Well-known Roman sites such as London (even with street-names supplied) were favoured 'sources'; on the Continent such places as Köln acted as similar magnets. Complete vessels of 'foreign' appearance or dubious date may be singled out, like the 'Wroxeter' cup (fig. 27.10), a Late Italian sigillata plate and an African dish, both from 'Köln' (pl. 17 top and fig. 22.2), and some unduly early terra sigillata stamps from 'Threadneedle St.

Plate 38 Expansion – early 19th century. *Top*: Burgoyne Collection: lion-head handle of a bowl. Athenian, 4th century AD. *Left*: Lord Elgin's Collection: amphora, North African *spatheion* type. 5th to early 6th century AD. Height 90 cm. (See also fig. 10.2 for detail.)
Bottom: Towneley Collection: early Arretine-ware plate, stamped A.TITI FIGV(L) four times (see also fig. 13.1). The white 'T' marking stands for 'Towneley', and the printed label refers to Walters' published *Catalogue*.
About 30–20 BC (scale *c.* 2:3, stamps 0.8 × 0.65 cm).

Plate 39 *Opposite page*: Spoils of Empire and war.
Top: flagon, collected by (Earl) Kitchener in Cyprus. Eastern Sigillata A ware, *c.* AD 1–50. Height 15.8 cm.
Bottom: plate, 'from the Somme', acquired during the First World War. An Italian Sigillata plate of late type, showing stamp (of *planta pedis* form, here Q.TERV), rouletting, and applied ornaments on the outside, *c.* AD 30–70.
Diam. of rim 15.2 cm.

[London]'. Among Walters' eleven pieces of Italian Sigillata stated to be British finds (his L 159–69), some are dubious, others (e.g. fig. 15.4 = L 161) are late products and could well have arrived as isolated imports after AD 43. Such pieces need to be approached with an open mind, since properly excavated material also includes the occasional freak import.

Plate 40 Finds from modern excavations. Mug/jug of Athenian type from Anglo-Libyan dig at Benghazi, gift of the Libyan government, c. AD 350–450. Height 19.5 cm.

Endnotes

Introduction

1 See pp. 90–4 for more details. Roman and related pottery is in fact divided among five of the BM's Departments of Antiquities: Greek and Roman, Prehistoric and Romano-British, Egyptian, Western Asiatic, and Medieval and Later.

2 H.B. Walters, *Catalogue of the Roman Pottery in the Departments of Antiquities, British Museum* (London 1908).

3 *Journal of Roman Pottery Studies* (1988–, annually, issued by Oxbow Books, Oxford). A new comprehensive survey of Romano-British wares and other British finds is now available: P. Tyers, *Roman Pottery in Britain* (London 1996).

4 Rouletting is the term used for fine notches produced either by a rotating cogged wheel or by holding a vibrating blade to the surface of the pot.

5 Barbotine decoration consists of patterns created by squeezing liquid clay through a nozzle, in the manner of icing a cake.

6 Two contrasting approaches may be seen in R.J. Charleston, *Roman Pottery* (London 1955), and D.P.S. Peacock, *Pottery in the Roman World: An Ethnoarchaeological Approach* (London 1982).

7 See, for instance, D. Williams, *Greek Vases* (London 1985). For further aspects, see T. Rasmussen and N. Spivey (eds), *Looking at Greek Vases* (Cambridge 1991).

8 See for instance S. Walker and A. Burnett, *The Image of Augustus* (London 1981), and S. Walker, *Roman Art* (London 1991).

9 Another BM vessel from Egypt, a late amphora (EA 32617), is covered with Coptic texts.

10 I here exclude mention of commercial amphorae, which were traded on account of their contents – again, some types are particularly widespread.

11 Pliny, *Natural History* XXXV.12 (46).160. Most of those noted by him remain uninvestigated.

12 H. Cockle, *Journal of Roman Studies* 71 (1981), 87–97.

Amphorae

13 The word is a Latin borrowing of the Greek term *amphoreus*.

14 One *amphora* = just under 26 litres. Most actual Roman vessels fall well short of this capacity.

15 For listings of these, and indications of their contents, see most recently A.J. Parker, *Ancient Shipwrecks of the Mediterranean and the Roman Provinces*, BAR S-580 (Oxford 1992).

16 For stamps on Roman amphorae, see M.H. Callender, *Roman Amphorae* (London 1965); also E.L. Will, in A.M. McCann, *The Roman Port and Fishery of Cosa* (Princeton 1987), 170–220.

17 Some good examples of these have been published from Masada, Israel: see H.M. Cotton and J. Geiger, *Masada II, The Latin and Greek Documents* (Jerusalem 1989).

18 H. Dressel, *Corpus inscriptionum latinarum* XV.ii.1 (Berlin 1899).

19 D.P.S. Peacock and D.F. Williams, *Amphorae and the Roman Economy* (London 1986).

20 See S.A. Castle, *Britannia* 9 (1978), 383–92.

21 Berytus type: Peacock and Williams 1986, class 12. Lipari type: Peacock and Williams 1986, class 13 (see also R.J.A. Wilson in *Archaeological Reports* 1995–96, 82, fig. 15 for new kiln finds). A few examples of both of these types reached Britain.

Fine wares

22 See P. Bernardini, *Museo Nazionale Romano: Le ceramiche* V.1 (Rome 1986).

23 These mimic decorated metalware: see for example the silver bowl, pl. 13 *bottom*. Most later Roman relief wares do the same.

24 The date of these has been a good deal discussed; for the earlier evidence, see M.T. Marabini Moevs, in *Memoirs of the American Academy in Rome* XXXIV (Rome 1980), 161–227, with 23 plates following. Examples are present on the Sant Jordi I shipwreck (Majorca), which is dated *c.* 100–90 BC. See Parker 1992. Further comments are provided by S.I. Rotroff, in *Journal of Roman Archaeology* 9 (1996), 316–20.

25 D. Atkinson, *Journal of Roman Studies* 4 (1914), 27–64.

26 For a recent study of a minor centre, which produced other fine wares also, see G. Pucci *et al.*, *La fornace di Umbricio Cordo* (Florence

1992). This lies in a rural area between Arezzo and Chiusi.

27 La Graufesenque and Banassac products.

28 Actually found in London.

29 The current terminology in various languages is presented in E. Ettlinger *et al.*, *Conspectus*, pp. 45ff.

30 A small version of this is seen in fig. 21.2. *top.*

Lead- and alkaline-glazed wares

31 The 'Aswan'-ware pot (fig. 25.1) apparently copies such a fritware shape.

Thin-walled wares, etc.

32 Provincial products are here represented by pl. 24 *bottom left*, and the Egyptian derivatives, fig. 28 *bottom*. Examples from Tharros (Sardinia) in the British Museum's collections (including pl. 24 *top*) are now published in some detail in R.D. Barnett and C. Mendleson, *Tharros: A Catalogue of Material in the British Museum* (London 1987). Compare (for these) M. Pinna, *Studi Sardi* 26 (1981–5), 239–302.

33 A late version of these, with ribbed and slashed treatment, appears in pl. 40.

34 For these, see I. Nicolaou, *Bulletin de correspondance hellénique* 113 (1989), 301–18.

Coarse wares

35 Tripolitanian, Sardinian and Cypriot (?) versions respectively.

36 Glass urns were, however, in more common use.

37 Inv. 1885.10–11.1, found at Bordighera (on display in the Wolfson Gallery).

Appendix

38 A brief general history of the British Museum and its collections can be found in M. Caygill, *The Story of the British Museum* (London 1981).

39 I hope to illustrate some of these in a forthcoming book.

40 See fig. 3.1, a Jordanian gift to Princess Michael of Kent.

41 In terms of sources, Turkey and Spain are under-represented; wares from the former French colonial areas of North Africa and Syria – common in French collections – are here mostly illustrated by examples found elsewhere.

Select bibliography

General works
M. Beltrán Lloris, *Cerámica romana. Tipología y clasificacion* (2 vols., Zaragoza 1978). Reproduces drawings from classic works. Useful bibliography, but many authors' names are misprinted.

R.J. Charleston, *Roman Pottery* (London 1955).

(Enciclopedia dell'arte antica,) Atlante delle forme ceramiche romane I, II (Rome 1981, 1985/6).

Rei Cretariae Romanae Fautorum Acta 1– (various imprints, from 1958). Specialist journal on Roman pottery studies; largely conference papers.

P. Lévèque and J.-P. Morel (eds) *Céramiques hellénistiques et romaines* I– (Besançon 1980, 1987, and forthcoming). Surveys of various categories.

British Museum works
O.M. Dalton, *Catalogue of Early Christian Antiquities in the British Museum* (London 1901).

C. Johns, *Arretine and Samian Pottery* (London 1971). Short guide.

H.B. Walters, *Catalogue of the Roman Pottery in the Departments of Antiquities, British Museum* (London 1908). The fundamental catalogue.

S. Walker, *Roman Art* (London 1991). A general overview.

Amphorae
D.P.S. Peacock and D.F. Williams, *Amphorae and the Roman Economy: An Introductory Guide* (London 1986).

M. Sciallano and P. Sibella, *Amphores. Comment les identifier?* (Édisud, Aix-en-Provence 1991; 2nd ed. 1994).

Rome, Republican fine wares
P. Bernardini, *Museo Nazionale Romano: Le ceramiche* V.1, *La ceramica a vernice nera dal Tevere* (Rome 1986). Finds from the Tiber banks – all major categories, with bibliography.

Hellenistic wares in the East
J.W. Hayes, 'Fine wares in the Hellenistic world', in T. Rasmussen and N. Spivey (eds) *Looking at Greek Vases* (Cambridge 1991), 183–202.

J.K. Papadopoulos, 'A Pergamene cup with *schemata sunousiastika*', in A. Cambitoglou (ed.), *Classical Art in the Nicholson Museum, Sydney* (Mainz 1995), 223–35, pls. 72–3. Erotic motifs.

Terra sigillata

E. Ettlinger *et al.*, *Conspectus formarum terrae sigillatae italico modo confectae* (*Materialien zur römisch-germanischen Keramik* 10) (Frankfurt and Bonn 1990).

A. Oxé and H. Comfort, *Corpus vasorum arretinorum* (Bonn 1968). Listings of potters' stamps on Italian Sigillata.

C. Bémont and J.-P. Jacob (eds), *La terre sigillée gallo-romaine* (*Documents d'Archéologie Française* 6) (Paris 1986). A survey of production centres in Gaul.

Terra sigillata: relief decorated vessels and moulds

A. Vannini, *Museo Nazionale Romano: Le ceramiche* V.2, *Matrici di ceramica aretina decorata* (Rome 1988).

C. Troso, *Il ceramista aretino Publius Cornelius. La produzione decorata a rilievo* (Pubblicazioni della Facoltà di Lettere e Filosofia dell'Università di Pavia 63) (Florence 1991). Decorated products of one large workshop (listing material in Arezzo).

M. Medri, *Terra sigillata tardo italica decorata* (Rome 1992), and C. Rossetti Tella, *La terra sigillata tardo-italica decorata del Museo Nazionale Romano* (Rome 1996). Two studies of the decorated 'Late Italian' class, offering rival classifications.

Fakes of same

F.P. Porten Palange, 'Fälschungen in der arretinischen Reliefkeramik', *Archäologisches Korrespondenzblatt* 19.1 (1989), 91–9, pls. 20–3.

Eastern Sigillata B ware versions of the above

S. Zabehlicky-Scheffenegger, 'Subsidiary factories of Italian Sigillata potters: the Ephesian evidence', in H. Koester (ed.), *Ephesos, Metropolis of Asia: An Interdisciplinary Approach*, Harvard Theological Studies 41 (Valley Forge, PA 1995) 217–28. Summarises longer reports in German by an Austrian team.

Lead-glazed wares (and associated kiln fittings)

A. Hochuli-Gysel, *Kleinasiatische glasierte Reliefkeramik (50 v. Chr. bis 50n. Chr.) und ihre oberitalischen Nachahmungen* (Acta Bernensia VII) (Bern 1977). Identifications now in need of revision.

N. Atik, *Die Keramik aus den Südthermen von Perge, Istanbuler Mitteilungen*, Beiheft 40 (Tübingen 1995), esp. pp. xix–xx, 1–58, pls. 1–11 for Perge finds. The Mytilene finds are still not formally published; most of Hochuli-Gysel's 'Smyrna' category (see the work cited above) should come from this source.

Pompeii, etc.
A. Carandini (ed.), *L'instrumentum domesticum di Ercolano e Pompei nella prima età imperiale, Quaderni di cultura materiale* 1 (Rome 1977).

Late Roman wares
J.W. Hayes, *Late Roman Pottery* (London 1972), with *Supplement* (1980).
P. Reynolds, *Trade in the Western Mediterranean, AD 400–700: The Ceramic Evidence*, BAR S-604 (Oxford 1995).

'Toy' pigs
G. Messineo, 'Puerilia crepitacula?', *Rivista di Studi Pompeiani* 5 (1991–2, published 1994), 119–32.

Finds of Mediterranean wares from sites in Britain
P. Tyers, *Roman Pottery in Britain* (London 1996), 85–105, 111–12, 121–2, 152–8 (amphorae, fine wares, mortaria).
P. Arthur, 'Roman Amphorae from Canterbury', *Britannia* 17 (1986), 239–58 (with references cited).
D. Williams and C. Carreras, 'North African amphorae in Roman Britain: a re-appraisal', *Britannia* 26 (1995), 231–52.

Gazetteer of shipwreck finds
A.J. Parker, *Ancient Shipwrecks of the Mediterranean and the Roman Provinces*, BAR S-580 (Oxford 1992).

Transition to Middle Ages
L. Paroli (ed.), *La ceramica invetriata tardoantica e altomedievale in Italia* (Florence 1992).

Clay analyses and identification of sources
G. Olcese (ed.), *Ceramica romana e archeometria: lo stato degli studi*, conference papers (Montegufoni 1993) = *Quaderni del Dipartimento di Archeologia, Università di Siena* 37 (Florence 1994/95).

(Excavation site reports are extensively cited in the works listed.)

Index of items illustrated

INVENTORY NUMBERS

British Museum Departmental codes: EA indicates Egyptian Antiquities, MLA Medieval and Later Antiquities, PRB Prehistoric and Romano-British, WA Western Asiatic. Items without code letters are in Greek and Roman Antiquities. Objects currently on display are marked with an asterisk. In recent years, when an object has been transferred, a new number indicating the transfer date has been assigned by the receiving Department. Old running Departmental numbers are also cited for Egyptian and Western Asiatic objects; 'K', 'L', 'M', etc. refer to the series in the older definitive Museum publications (e.g. Walters' *Catalogue*), often cited in the specialist literature. For Dalton, see bibliography. Place-names appearing in parentheses indicate known find-spots.

COLOUR PLATES

(* indicates that the object is on display in the Wolfson Gallery,
** in the new Hellenistic Gallery)

I   EA 54362

II   *1902.10–12.2 [L 35]; 1814.7–4.1554 [L 136]; 1869.2–5.4 [L 54];
1873.8–20.328 [M 1]; 1866.6–8.2 [L 123] (= Walker, fig. 76)

III *EA 35993 (1868.11–2.113)

IV   *Left*: EA 65437 [1950.5–20.2]. *Centre*: GR 1906.10–22.1.
Right: EA 59871 [1930.7–14.5]

V   *Left*: *1888.11–15.8 [K 6 – Leventis Gallery]. *Right*: 1900.7–27.6
[K 36]

VI   *Left*: EA 37540. *Right*: EA 26820

VII *EA 21712 [1888.5–12.182]

PLATES

1 *Top*: 1868.1–10.756. *Left*: 1980.10–14.5. *Bottom left*: 1856.12–23.404.
Bottom right: 1856.12–23.379

2 EA 27718 [1877.11–12.86ff.]

3 *Left*: 1987.4–2.1 [Q 2086 *bis*: see Bailey, *BM Catalogue Lamps* IV (1996),
132, pls. 173, 179]

4 1900.7–26.5 [L 107]: mould on right, cast on left

5 *Top*: *1866.6–8.2. *Right*: 1856.10–4.234

6 **1898.11–21.2

7 *Left*: EA 22402 [1885.11–1.274]. *Centre*: EA 22181 [1885.11–1.247].
Right: EA 22379 [1885.11–1.295]

8 *Left*: *1899.12–19.1. *Right*: *1904.2–4.1451

9 *Left*: *1859.2–16.12. *Right*: EA 22364 [1885.11–1.156?]

10 *Left*: EA 53955 [1915.2–7.5]. *Right*: WA 48333 [1880.5–1.31]

11 *Top*: *1756.1–1.904. *Left*: *1904.6–1.2

12 *1873.2–8.3 [G 28]

13 *Top*: *1839.11–9.23. *Bottom*: **1989.7–24.1

14 *From left, clockwise*: *1856.12–23.378 [L 48]; *1856.12–23.366 (Tharros);
*1981.12–18.2 (formerly Victoria & Albert Museum 1929–1901);
*1857.1–6.7. *Centre*: *1859.12–26.327. *Bottom*: *1868.6–20.263 (= Walker,
fig. 78)

15 1980.10–14.8

16 *Top*: 1915.12–8.53. *Left*: EA 51547 [1912.11–9.401] (fig. 2)

17 *Top*: 1910.10–11.4. *Left*: PRB, uninv. (= pl. 19.5)

18 (1) 1915.12–29.4. (2) 1847.8–6.62 (=fig. 15.3). (3) 1904.2–4.888. (4)
1980.10–14.8. (5) 1856.12–23.392. (6) 1814.7–4.1557.

19 (1) 1873.8–20.515. (2) 1853.5–2.24 [L 159]. (3) PRB uninv. ('U 32').
(4) 1893.5–24.8, L 70]. (5) PRB, uninv. (=pl. 17 *left*)

20 *Left*: 1853.5–28.62 (Tarsus). *Right*: 1848.8–4.69 (see fig. 21.3 *bottom*)

21 *MLA 1986.7–1.1, 2, 3, 4

22 *Top*: *MLA 1928.4–13.8. *Bottom left*: *MLA 1928.4–13.9 (see Hayes, *Late Roman Pottery*, pl. XIVb). *Bottom right*: *MLA 1986.7–1.11

23 1856.12–23.406 [K 17] (=Barnett and Mendleson, *Tharros*, 238, pls. 21 and 137)

24 *Top, left to right*: 1856.12–23.345, 344, 359 and 339 (= Barnett and Mendleson, *Tharros*, 243–4, pls. 20, 142). *Bottom left*: 1905.5–20.139. *Bottom right*: 1985.10–14.2 (ex 1888.12–18.714)

25 *Left*: 1868.6–20.249. *Right*: 1963.12–22.1

26 *Top*: *1849.6–20.8 [G 186]. *Bottom*: 1857.12–20.169; 1868.6–20.266

27 *Top*: 1933.6–13.1 (Rhodes). *Bottom*: EA 37631

28 *Left*: EA 5242. *Bottom left*: 1856.12–23.204. *Bottom right*: 1859.11–29.9

29 1860.10–2.24.

30 EA 22179; EA 42121 (Esna)

31 1860.10–2.56

32 *Top*: 1856.12–26.392 (Puteoli). *Bottom*: 1893.7–13.86; 1859.12–26.556

33 1990.1–27.1, 2, 4 (glass), 3, 5 (lamp)

34 *From top left, clockwise*: 1868.6–20.228; 1856.12–26.536; 1868.1–5.2 (small); 1856.12–26.538; 1951.9–7.3; 1888.9–20.54

35 *1888.9–20.47

36 *Right*: *MLA 1875.10–12.16 [Dalton, no. 860]. *Bottom left*: *MLA 1882.1–9.1 [Dalton, no. 903]. *Bottom right*: *MLA 1891.4–14.10 [Dalton, no. 908]

37 *Left*: 1756.1–1.1014 [K 63]. *Right*: 1756.1–1.1132

38 *Top*: 1842.7–28.9 (Athens). *Left*: 1816.6–10.257 [Money Gallery]. *Right*: 1814.7–4.1559 [L 128]

39 *Top*: *1982.7–29.59 (formerly Victoria & Albert Museum 339–1883; from Salamis, Cyprus). *Bottom*: 1917.10–15.2

40 *1975.2–7.2

FIGURES

1 (1) 1949.5–1.5 (Tintagel); (2) MLA 1985.7–1.83 (Istanbul); (3) 1949.5–1.9; (4) MLA 1985.7–1.75

2 EA 51547 [1912.11–9.401] (Faras)

3 (1) WA 139025 [1977.11–2.2] ('Petra'); (2) 1977.10–11.9 (Knidos, old find: Newton), 1864.10–7.1359 (Ephesos)

4 (1) EA 22387 [1888.9–20.55]; (2) EA 22181 [1885.11–1.247], base detail; (3) EA 5110 [1837.7–14.15B]

5 1900.7–26.5 [L 107] (Arezzo)

6 1936.7–20.1 [Q 1009]

7 1917.10–15.2 (Somme valley)

8 (1) 1965.3–22.2; (2) 1973.1–5.1

9 (1–3, 5) 1955.9–20.90, 89, 196, 169; (4) 1955.9–20.80; (6, 7) 1886.4–1.1703 (Naucratis); 1955.9–20.91; (8–10): 1857.10–15.3, 1, 6 (all Monte Testaccio, Rome)

10 (1) 1846.1–10.10 (Eppelsheim, Alzey); (2) 1816.6–10.257, rim (= pl. 38 *left*)

11 EA 22365 [1885.11–1.459]

12 (1) 1904.2–4.902; (2) 1867.11–22.388

13 (1) 1814.7–4.1559 [L 128]; 1915.12–29.4 (Rome)

14 (1) 1866.6–8.2 [L 123]; (2) 1904.2–4.888 [L 126] (Loriol); (3) 749 [L 124] (Loriol)

15 (1) 1873.8–20.515 [L 58] (see pl. 19); (2) 1865.12–14.40 [M 2]; (3) 1847.8–6.62 [L 55] (see pl. 18.2); (4) 1855.5–12.7 [L 161] ('London')

16 (1) 1904.2–4.1326 [L 172] (Orange); (2) PRB, uninv. base;

(3) 1857.8–4.20 [L 85]; (4) 1868.1–10.755 [L 4] (Corfu); (5) 1917.10–15.2
(Somme valley); (6) 1855.5–12.6 [L 164] ('London'); (7) 1910.10–11.4
('Köln'); (8) EA 5262; (9) 1856.12–26.557 [L 147] (Torre Annunziata).
Stamps: (1) CCRISPIN / PRI; (2) VETTI/OPTA; (4) CFAP(p);
(5) Q.TERV (see pl. 39 *bottom*); (7) LRPIS; (8) SEX.MCA; (9) AFL or AEL
(4–9 *in planta pedis*)

17 (1) 1909.3–20.23; (2) 1915.12–29.10 (Rome); (3) 1856.12–23.379 [L 44]
(Tharros); (4) 1909.3–20.2; (5) 1814.7–4.1553 [L 137]; (6) 1868.1–10.752;
(7) 1814.7–4.1554 [L 136]; (8) 1904.2–4.748 [M 33] (Vaison);
(9) 1856.12–23.381 (Tharros); (10) 1868.1–10.753 [L 6] (Corfu);
(11) 1814.7–4.1557 [L 142]. Stamps: (1) CMEM[mi] / PRIMVS;
(2) CRISPINI; (3) C.VIBIE[ni]; (4) POTVS / PCOR[neli]; (6) CNF;
(7) NAE / HVS?; (8) CRESTI; (10) LAVIL; (11) SEXMCL. (6, 10, 11 *in
planta pedis*)

18 EA 51512 [1912.11–9.365] (Faras)

19 (1) 1848.8–4.1 [L 8] (Kerch pen.); (2) 1868.6–20.261; (3) 1860.6–20.260;
(4) EA 22270 [1885.11–1.361]; (5) 1856.12–26.556 [L 135] (Torre
Annunziata); (6) 1872.4–5.205; (7) 1868.6–20.431

20 (1) 1848.8–4.15; (2) EA 22437 [1885.11–1.362]; (3) 1853.5–28.67;
(4) 1853.5–28.63 [L 36] (Tarsus); (5) 1853.5–28.71; (6) 1876.9–9.40
(Cyprus); (7) EA 5255; (8) 1853.5–28.69; (9) 1894.11–1.512

21 *Top*: (1) 1881.8–24.70; (2) 1896.2–1.258 (Kourion); (3) 1880.7–10.70.
Bottom: (1) 1877.8–5.2 [L 15]; (2) 1856.10–4.139; (3) 1848.8–4.69 (stamp:
pl. 20 *right*)

22 (1) Towneley Coll., PRB not inv. [M 2405]; (2) 1920.11–18.25 ('Köln');
(3) 1856.12–23.403 (Tharros); (4) 1965.12–13.1; (5) 1856.12–23.401
(Tharros); (6) 1859.11–29.10 (Karpathos); (7) 1928.4–13.8 (Egypt?);
(8) EA 37413 [1902.10–11.112]; (9) 1857.12–18.164; (10) 1928.4–13.10
(Egypt?); (11) EA 5258; (12) EA 69381 [1982.5–26.131, formerly Victoria
& Albert Museum, 472–1891]; (13) EA 50654 [1861.7–24.1] (Wadi Faran,
Sinai); (14) EA 27718 [1877.11–12.86ff.] (= pl. 2; also fig. 25.6)

23 1985.10–14.1

24 1911.10–18.4

25 (1) EA 5129; (2) EA 58677 [1927.2–12.2]; (3) *EA 36036 [1875.7–20.2];
(4) EA 59555 [1929.10–16.129]; (5) EA 50634 [1911.7–10.60];
(6) EA 27718; (7) EA 51498 [1912.11–9.391] (Faras); (8) 1928.4–13.11;
(9) *1888.9–20.41 (two views)

26 1956.2–19.1

27 (1) 1839.11–9.14B; (2) 1839.11–12.2; (3) 1814.7–4.656;
(4) 1873.8–20.333 [L 53]; (5) 1910.12–19.7; (6) 1980.10–14.6 (ex Victoria &
Albert Museum 1068–1905); (7) 1839.11–12.1; (8) EA 5252;
(9) 1935.6–10.3; (10) 1871.7–14.8 [M 2534] ('Wroxeter')

28 (1) 1961.2–13.4; (2) 1980.10–14.9; (3) EA 51638 [1912.11–9.496]
(Faras); (4) 1912.11–9.521 (Faras)

29 (1) 1859.12–26.323; (2) 1926.4–10.48

30 1933.6–13.1 (Rhodes)

31 (1) 1977.10–11.61; (2) 1856.12–26.392 (rim detail); (3) EA 5101;
(4) EA 5264; (5) 1975.2–7.3 (Benghazi); (6) 1975.2–7.5 (Benghazi);
(7) 1864.10–7.1936; (8) EA 5261; (9) EA 5257

32 (1) 1927.4–11.130 (Tanturah); (2) 1814.7–4.1118; (3) 1927.4–11.97
(Tanturah); (4) EA 5260; (5) EA 22381 [1885.11–1.296]

33 (1) 1927.4–11.128 (Tanturah Dor; one side restored);
(2) 1927.4–11.100 (Tanturah); (3) EA 22179 [1885.11–1.272] (rim detail)

34 (1) 1893.7–13.86; (2) 1921.12–20.117; (3) 1859.12–26.556 (Knidos)